YOUR BABY'S UGLY

MAXIMIZE THE VALUE OF YOUR BUSINESS OR YOU'LL HAVE NOTHING TO SELL

Thoughts on *Your Baby's Ugly*

Those who operate their own company, firm or practice typically plan for everything – except success. Too often, business owners focus only on generating an income from their operations; they fail to realize that the real payoff comes from building an enterprise that has value beyond the income they annually earn. The result is a squandered opportunity to truly achieve the American Dream. If you're a business owner and you want to avoid that mistake, read Your Baby is Ugly. This could be the best book on entrepreneurship I've ever read. It presents a highly realistic view of operating a business and offers practical advice that can make the difference between you selling your business one day for massive amounts of money – or failing to get even a single offer. The sooner you read this in the life cycle of your enterprise, the better.

—Ric Edelman, founder, Edelman Financial Engines, and author of *The Truth About Your Future*

To my team, I could not be here without you. I am so thankful for your commitment to helping me make finances simple.

ACKNOWLEDGMENTS

I'd like to extend a special thank you to Corporate Value Metrics and the CVGA instructors, Ken Sanginario – founder of Corporate Value Metrics, John Lawlor - founder of Practical Decisions, and Christine Hollinden – founder of Hollinden Marketing. Without a doubt, the Certified Value Growth Advisor (CVGA) training program of Corporate Value Metrics and CVM's Value Opportunity Profile (VOP) software has shaped my view of how to grow lasting value in business. I credit my education in value growth to the exceptional instruction by the CVGA faculty.

Even after 25 years of growing and selling businesses, this course and software created new and inspirational content for business value growth. If you are an advisor; I would highly encourage you to pursue the CVGA designation to further your own and your client's success. If you are a business owner, it is imperative to work with a CVGA licensed individual who understands the complexity and foundational importance of Value Growth.

The permissions granted to use CVGA and VOP copyrighted content extend to the inclusion of this book only. Any other use or reproduction of such content without the expressed written content of Corporate Value Metrics is prohibited.

ISBN: 978-1-954759-32-9 (Ebook)
ISBN: 978-1-954759-33-6 (paperback)
ISBN: 978-1-954759-34-3 (hardcover)

Ordering Information:
Special discounts are available on quantity purchases by corporations, associations, and others. For details, contact email info@financiallysimple.com. Cover image by Zdorov Kirill Vladimirovich / Shutterstock.com

CONTENTS

YOUR BABY'S UGLY

MAXIMIZE THE VALUE OF YOUR BUSINESS OR YOU'LL HAVE NOTHING TO SELL

JUSTIN A. GOODBREAD
CFP®, CEPA®, CVGA®

Foreword

After our owner-led tour of a large, machined-parts manufacturing facility, my business partner and I walked through the parking lot. We opened our car doors and, in sync, looked at one another. "Well," my partner began, "that baby was ugly."

I smiled back at him. I knew he was right. "Yeah, you're right," I replied. "But we need to remember that it is *his* ugly baby."

Imagine we are meeting for the first time. As we begin to share personal things about ourselves so that we can get to know each other, you tell me you have a daughter. You are so proud of your daughter. She is the light of your life. You tell me excitedly that she has just gotten married. You tell me how special the moment was when you escorted her down the center of the church to meet her future husband to exchange their vows. I empathize because I remember doing the same thing just a few years ago with my lovely daughter. We talk about what a wonderful mix of emotions we were feeling at that moment.

"She was absolutely beautiful on her wedding day," you say to me. You ask me if I would like to see a picture of your daughter.

"Of course," I enthusiastically respond.

You break out your phone, pop open your photos app, and tap the picture of your daughter in her wedding dress on her wedding day in the flower garden out in front of the church. Then you extend your arm toward my face to proudly show me your beautiful daughter.

"Wow, she is really ugly," I respond.

How would you feel? You probably would want to punch me in the nose. You certainly would be annoyed and think of me as a very rude and insensitive human being. Even if it were true that your daughter is ugly, she is still *your* ugly baby. I figure that would likely be the end of our relationship. That is what it is like when a buyer takes a look at your business and tells you your baby is ugly.

When a buyer looks at your business, they are strictly thinking, should I be getting a discount (because your baby is ugly), or should I be paying a premium (because your baby is beautiful)? The buyer has no emotional attachment to your baby just yet. But to you, that emotional attachment is deeply rooted. You know how hard you have worked to raise your baby. The good times and bad times, the trials and tribulations. Unless you are a business owner yourself, it is impossible to grasp the significance of this. There is so much that goes into owning a business. Business ownership is not just a financial journey and business journey. Owning a business is personal. Although a buyer is looking at your business in a rational way—in other words, discount or premium—most business owners are taking the buyer's evaluation of their business personally. This is my baby, and if it is a little ugly or even very ugly, you will show it some respect and show me some respect.

The machined-parts business my partner and I looked at was definitely ugly. Beginning with the financials, sales and profits had been down for three years in a row. Gross margins were low, forcing the owner to squeeze selling, general, and administrative expenses to eke out a profit. Receivables and payables were strung out as the owner tried to manage the cash flow. There was too much debt, and given the reduction in cash flow, the owner was having trouble balancing paying debt versus investing in the factory. The factory floor reflected this. It looked old and tired. It was messy, dirty, and unorganized. The raw materials were scattered. The warehouse was unorganized. Oh, and that pile of boxes back in the corner? Old, obsolete inventory the owner had not gotten around to getting rid of.

"Is it at least written off the books?" I asked.

"No," answered the owner. "Have not gotten around to that yet." The staff on the floor looked tired and unmotivated. Even the clothes they were wearing were dirty.

"We *are* in a machined-parts factory," my partner said to me.

"I realize that," I responded, "but there is still a difference. I wonder what the customers and employees all think about this?" Entering the owner's office, we could see papers strewn about the office. This owner was not only the president but also the controller, scheduler, and floor manager. In fact, the business was completely dependent on him. The reality was he was stuck and was unable to handle all the things that needed handling. He was always so reluctant to give up control. Yet here he was—he had almost completely lost control. Now granted, you are probably thinking right now that this is an extreme case. But is it?

The fact remains that only about 20 percent of the businesses that go to market actually result in a completed and successful sale. And only around 30 percent of family transitions succeed into the second generation.1 The numbers get even worse as the generations pass. Think about that. Only one in five businesses that go to market sell. And less than two of five family businesses make it to the second generation. What happens to the others? Tragedy. They most likely liquidate just like this machined-parts company ended up doing. And why is this the case? Because so many businesses are ugly. We spoil our ugly babies. We don't do the things we should be doing to make them attractive and ready to transition—in other words, get them ready to walk down the aisle.

But how do you know what to do? Where do you start? Start by reading Justin's book, *Your Baby's Ugly: Maximize the Value of Your Business, or You'll Have Nothing to Sell.*

One thing I love about his writing is his way of taking complex topics, simplifying them, and providing real, straightforward, and practical suggestions on how to build a better business and create wealth. Maybe this comes from his background as a business owner himself. In Justin's first book, *The Ultimate Sale: A Financially Simple Guide to Selling a Business for Maximum Profit,* Justin laid out, in his financially simple style, how to position your business to sell at a premium. But those of us who have been at the heart of reinventing the exit planning process, leaders like Justin, understand that exit planning is a business strategy first. It is what you do in your business every day that determines a successful outcome. If you operate your business with the end in mind, benefits will show their face not just down the road when it's time to transition your baby but also right away. You can have both.

In this book, Justin describes the eight areas of your business that not only position you for an ultimate sale but will set you up for growth in revenue and profits today. Forget about the exit for now. What can you do today to build a better business? Focus on the present. Exit planning is present tense. That means more sales, more profit, and more exit options. Read this book. Follow Justin's checklists. Put his words to action. And watch how beautiful your baby becomes.

Chris Snider
CEO, Exit Planning Institute
Author of *Walking to Destiny*

WHY

Why Your Baby Is Ugly

Son, you never tell a woman that her baby's ugly. But sometimes you have to. And if you do … you better run or duck!

When I was a young boy, my dad used to love making this joke. He would chuckle every time, which, in turn, made me laugh too.

The truth is, we business owners do keep a secret from the world. When the world sees a business owner, it sees success: a nicer house, a newer vehicle, exotic vacations, and the ability to set your own schedule.

What people often don't see is that *we are scared to death*. We're scared of harming the team that we know, love, and trust. We're afraid that losing one of our team members might put the business in a tailspin. We're cautiously terrified of risk, the possibility of bankruptcy, the potential of losing that big customer, or missing out on the next deal.

The worry keeps us up at night. I speak with business owners all over the country, and they text me at 4:00 a.m. while they're out taking a walk, telling me that they're praying for their employees and customers. That's the deep, dark secret business owners carry.

During our younger years, we push on with excitement. We push toward an idea of "success," but at some point, it happens— life or business kicks us in the teeth. And before we know it, we find ourselves flat on our back, wondering what happened. Look at something like the COVID-19 pandemic: it has caused many business owners to question whether it's wise to even *be* in business. As business owners, we're pouring a ton of time and resources into the company only to, many times, have apparent success thrown back in our face by our employees or our customers. And we know all too well how it feels to have somebody attack us and our vision.

So, What's the Solution?

We hold onto the idea that there'll be a pot of gold at the end of the proverbial rainbow when we eventually decide to sell our business. That's what we imagine. But, as we will cover in this book, that is, statistically, not the case.[2] The business that keeps us up at night, that we pour all our time and energy into, is often not sellable.

It's an ugly baby. It's our baby, and we love it, and we try to defend it, and we are very possessive about it, but that doesn't change the reality of the situation. It's comparable to Dr. Frankenstein creating his monster, right? As Mary Shelley's story goes, Frankenstein created his "baby," and ultimately, he had to destroy it. So, you read books and seek advice from friends on how to bring your company more *value*.

As a small business owner, you recognize that *v* word. You know the time and money you've invested in your company is valuable. True, some of your equipment or technologies may be valuable. But is your *company* valuable? Are you creating something valuable to others, or is it only valuable to you? Suppose you want your company to become a marketplace leader to receive money from investors, or to sell your business for profit. In that case, **you must understand what makes your business valuable to others**. Then, you'll want to work to grow the value of your business.

Now, more than a few of us have learned from past mistakes. Others have overcome some of life's obstacles, and we have a little bit more gusto.

But the reality of the situation is that our baby is ugly. It's unlikely that we're going to be able to sell our baby. We're ultimately not going to be able to reap the rewards of our years of effort to the extent that we want to.

I learned this lesson myself as a novice owner of a small landscaping company. I was working 80 hours a week for myself so that I didn't have to work 40 hours a week for "the man." Yet, all I seemed to do was earn enough money to pay my bills. I was working day in and day out without realizing any value growth. My business had grown stagnant, and I wanted advice on how to grow my company's value. I desired to increase my sales and revenue, but I didn't want to make mistakes that would hurt my business.

I Didn't Understand at the Time That My Baby Was Ugly

I needed help making business decisions, so I sought professional guidance. In my ignorance, I scheduled an appointment with some financial advisors at a national firm, only for them to tell me, "If you don't have any money to invest, we can't help you." They were a *little* more diplomatic than that, but that's what they meant. Next, I turned to the accounting world and met with certified public accountants for business advice. Still, they were only interested in completing my tax returns or keeping my books in order. They offered a little bit of insight into how and when to make moves in my business, but, man, I needed more than that.

I ended up turning to a business coach who, I later discovered, had never actually owned a business. That person had me focus on my mission and vision but did little to affect my business's value.

After some searching, I discovered people who knew exactly what I needed to do to grow my small business. However, these consultants and advisors were too busy working with much larger companies that brought in $30 million, $50 million, or $100 million a year in revenue. And here I was, just a small-business owner turning my first little bit of profit to feed my family, knowing that I was missing something significant in the game of business. Realizing that I wasn't going to get the help I needed without paying more than I could afford, I began to educate myself.

Through my years of consulting with thousands of business owners, I discovered these struggles are pervasive. Business owners everywhere seek to learn how to increase their companies' value and, ultimately, their net worth. They read books, go to seminars, and seek peer advice, all the while hiding the fact that they don't have a clue what they are doing.

Now my companies have grown into industry leaders because of the knowledge and experience I've gained.

Value vs. Profit

I've learned that whether a business grows and is sellable comes down to one question. This one question can redefine how you view your existing company and what you do with it:

Do you want to grow a company that is *profitable* or one that is *valuable*?

This distinction matters. Just because you increase the company's cash flow, which could increase its profitability, doesn't mean that you've decreased the **company-specific risk**. Throughout the book, I will talk through company-specific risk, but for now, keep in mind that **the lower the risk, the higher the value**. In the pages and chapters to come, I'll show you why you should focus on value rather than profitability if you want to take your business to the next level.

Eight Core Areas

During my formal training to earn the certified value growth advisor (CVGA) credential and my 25-plus years of owning and advising companies, I have learned there are eight core areas of business that can help you add value to your company: **planning**, **leadership**, **sales**, **marketing**, **people**, **operations**, **finance**, and **legal**. We're going to dive into each of these areas and highlight how to apply them—this process, known as **strategic planning**, is one that organizations use to set objectives and follow through on completing them.

If you focus on growing the value of your small business, your company can rise to the pinnacle of the marketplace. You can build a best-in-class business! You can attract investors! Additionally, you can position your business in such a way that you can **sell it for profit**. But it won't happen overnight. The process of value growth takes time and energy and an in-depth understanding of value and valuation.

If you don't build best-in-class businesses, if you don't dress up your baby, if you don't get your baby in a position where it can live without you, your baby will cry and fuss and make messes that are difficult to clean up. You want a break! You want a babysitter so you have some time for yourself. You want to be able to focus your energies on the things that matter most to you. You want your baby to flourish and have a great life.

Your baby is ugly—right now. But that can change if you follow these steps.

CHAPTER 1

Value: Your Baby Should Be Worth Every Penny

You are a firefighter!

Yes, if you are like most business owners, your day is spent running around putting out fires. You're often so involved with day-to-day dilemmas that you lose sight of why you're in business, or you lose sight of your business's potential. Usually, when you lose objectivity, you forget to plan ahead. You worry about making money *now* rather than growing money for your future.

You want your business to be profitable. But often you seek profitability to the detriment of your family, reinvesting every single dime back into your company for the promise of a future golden goose. You see, small business owners can become so focused on making a profit that they forget about other areas of their businesses and their personal lives. And, when pressed, many business owners view their businesses as their "retirement ticket," thinking that a buyer will swoop in and write them a big fat check for their money-making machine. But maximizing value is about a lot more than just selling your business and retiring—it's about creating a highly transferable business, a business that provides your dream lifestyle without the stresses of the average business owner.

If you create a company that's high in value, people will want it. But that doesn't mean you have to sell it! At the same time, if you don't build a company that's high in value, when it comes time to sell it, you're not going to be offered the amount of money you need to make the return of your investment into your business worthwhile. Why? Because your baby will be ugly to everyone but you!

According to a 2018 study, about one-third of business owners (32 percent) plan to sell their companies within two years. The updated 2020 Insight Report by BizBuySell tells us that "fifty-four percent of brokers expect the business-for-sale market to return to pre-pandemic levels within a year, something owners should consider when evaluating timelines."[3] Knowing about this potential flood of sellers and the massive number of businesses going to market, I ask this question: is your company worth buying?

A lifelong friend of mine reached out to me for help after I earned my certified exit planning advisor (CEPA) designation. Let's call him Jeff. So, Jeff called me and asked me to help him with his personal finances and business planning. Ultimately, he wanted me to help him position himself to sell his business. Now, Jeff is what you'd consider a successful entrepreneur. He had new cars, a new house, a fancy boat, and multiple employees, and he often traveled. Jeff had spent his business career making his company profitable, and he'd done a good job of it.

For all intents and purposes, Jeff was successful. However, he had a problem: most of Jeff's net worth was locked up in his business. He reinvested most of his profits from his company back into equipment or other items he needed to turn higher profits. It was a vicious cycle. Jeff could tell me about the cost and efficiency of each piece of equipment he purchased over the years, but his actual business wasn't worth anything. Sure, Jeff produced a nice income for his family's consumption, but he didn't have a business worth buying or retirement funds to sustain him in the future.

Jeff's business wasn't the retirement ticket he anticipated or desired it to be. Rather than investing money into other income-producing assets like retirement accounts, real estate, or other businesses, Jeff had invested his extra money back into his business. Now the only thing he could sell was his equipment, which would provide him only pennies on his dollar. He was stuck! Jeff, the "successful" business owner, had reached the place many seasoned business owners find themselves. He realized that profitability did not equal value. Even though he had a profitable business, it wasn't an asset of value that someone else would want to buy or invest in. Although his business was profitable, it was not valuable. It provided for his present but didn't secure his future.

Having a profitable business is vital to your company's survival and its attractiveness to potential investors and buyers. However, if *profits* are the only thing you seek to improve, then *other areas* of your business will suffer. Trying to save money, you may hire employees with average skills to avoid paying higher salaries for employees with exceptional skills. Trying to keep your profit margins high, you may keep outdated equipment or antiquated tech systems in place that hamper your operations instead of investing in state-of-the-art equipment. Although you're keeping your expenses low and your income high, you're neglecting other fundamental areas of your business.

Another issue is what I call the *lie of profitability*. Have you ever met a business owner who appears to have everything: time, money, trips, cars, and boats? I meet them often. Their company is providing them with a fantastic cash flow, **but it's a lie!** Allow me to illustrate. Let's say that your business grosses $1 million in annual sales. And for simplicity, let's say that the owner pays themself $300,000 a year and uses the business for other perks like company trips and a company car, equaling an annual package of $400,000. If the company were to sell for $3 million, then the business owner would need a 13.33 percent return on the proceeds of the business sale to maintain the lifestyle they've created. This isn't very probable. And if we incorporate the taxes associated with the business's sale, the $3 million sales proceeds would be reduced, causing the 13.33 percent return on proceeds to eclipse 20 percent, or even more.

So, I reiterate—**focusing on profitability has created a lie**.

The Somber Truth

You can break privately held businesses into three segments:[4]

1. **Micro-market,** with revenues under $5 million
2. **Lower-middle market,** with revenues between $5 million and $100 million
3. **Upper-middle market and large companies,** with revenues above $100 million

According to a private market study done by the Pepperdine Private Capital Markets Project and Key Private Bank, about 250,000 business owners in the lower-middle market (businesses that gross between $5 million and $100 million annually) were expected to exit by 2030.[5] Those trends were emerging even before the coronavirus pandemic brought about economic issues in 2020.

One big reason for that trend is baby boomers—the influential generation born between 1946 and 1964. Millions of business owners are baby boomers,[6] and by 2030 every single baby boomer will have reached retirement age. The baby boomers' demographic shift to retirement is known as a "gray tsunami," and will have a significant impact on our society.[7]

Beyond baby boomers, many business owners who had visions of an early retirement saw setbacks due to the great recession of 2007–2009. Their businesses suffered, and if they didn't have assets outside of those businesses, it set many peoples' exit plans back another five or 10 years.

Here's where it gets scary: according to the Exit Planning Institute, only about 50,000 among those 250,000 businesses that are going to be offered for sale in the next decade will be market ready. Many business owners will think they're ready to sell their companies, but when they visit a broker or an investment bank, that expert will look at the businesses and tell the owners they have work to do. Among that group of market-ready businesses, only 30,000 will actually transact—meaning there's a 40 percent transaction failure rate among business owners who want to sell their companies. Therefore, 40 percent of those who think they're ready to sell won't be able to.

Those are dreams that don't come true.

It gets worse. Out of those 30,000 who do sell, about 16,000 will sell with concessions, meaning that more than half of those who sell will not sell at the value the business owner wants. That leaves around 14,000 businesses that will sell at the desired value. To put that another way—of those 250,000 business owners who desire to sell in the next decade or so, only about 5–6 percent will be completely satisfied with what they get. And that's only for the businesses that sell—most won't.

The numbers are even more dismal in the micro market (businesses with less than $5 million annual gross)! **If you are part of the 5.3 million business owners in the micro market, you should take serious note of this information.**

I don't know about you, but I find these figures depressing. When I provide a business owner with these, I frequently hear a story about a competitor of theirs who sold their company for five times the EBIT (Earnings Before Interest and Taxes), or five times the revenue, or five times the EBITDA (Earnings Before Interest, Tax, Depreciation, and Amortization), and so on. But those numbers and scenarios could be manipulated or totally different from the way you're operating your business. Believing a statement of fact from someone without knowing the full details can cause a business owner to think their business is more valuable or attractive than it really is.

A Tale of Two Companies

Let's look further into the difference between profitability and value by examining two different companies.

Company A and Company B have the exact same products and services. They've both been operating for 20 years and are in the same industry. Each is producing $5 million in sales and has $500,000 in EBITDA. They're both experiencing the same nominal market growth. On the surface, they seem to have the same value. But they don't.

A TALE OF 2 COMPANIES

COMPANY A	COMPANY B
$5 million in sales & $500,000 EBITDA	$5 million in sales & $500,000 EBITDA
Has no strategic planning in place	Has a highly developed strategic plan in place
Has no Customer Relationship Management systems (CRMs)	Has advanced Customer Relationship Management Systems (CRMs)
Has some outdated technology and software systems in place	Has newer, state-of-the-art technology and software systems in place
Has no financial reporting or financial forecasting capabilities	Has up-to-date financial reporting and forecasting capabilities
Has no product development	Has robust product development
Has worn equipment	Has pristine equipment
Has a weak management team	Has an outstanding management team
Has little to no employee training	Has extensive employee training capabilities and regimens

We need to look further into each company to understand why they don't have the same value. Let's look at their differences.

In a side-by-side comparison, which company is more valuable? The companies have the same sales and revenue, but which company would you *invest in*? Would you buy Company A, which has no product development, worn-out equipment, no strategic planning, old systems, unreliable financial reporting, and little employee training? Or would you buy Company B, which has robust research and development, pristine equipment, highly developed strategic planning, state-of-the-art systems, disciplined financials, and an expertly trained team? That's a no-brainer, right?

Don't Be Like Jeff

Instead of building valuable companies like Company B, small-business owners tend to chase profits like Company A. They try to drive up revenue and bottom-line profits—the **quantitative** measures. Don't misunderstand me—please know that I'm not telling you to ignore profits. What I'm saying is that chasing quantitative results *alone* can negatively affect your organization. Because you need the revenue, you often focus on quantitative results, but if you want your company to be profitable for you *and* valuable to others, you need to focus on your company's **qualitative** values.

If you focus on driving the value (the qualitative) up, then profitability (the quantitative) tends to follow. And maybe, just maybe, you could see an unimaginable increase in profits and position your business to become a publicly traded company or to sell for a profit in the future.

Friends, value and profitability are two different things. Don't be like Jeff, who spent his whole life trying to drive up profits by working only on his business's quantitative areas. Additionally, don't be like other business owners I see who drive up profits but don't save any money outside of their businesses. You may not want to sell your company, or you may not have a company that will sell. That's fine. Nonetheless, you can position your company in such a way that you are financially independent from it personally. You can increase its value and profitability to save money for your future retirement.

Collecting Value for Your Business

To illustrate value, I want to take you back to my elementary school days when I started investing in baseball cards—those pieces of cardboard with players' photos and stats on them. My dad and I would go to the store each week, and I'd spend my hard-earned money to buy more cards for my collection. Once we got home, we'd open up the pack, and we'd look through the *Beckett Price Guide* to see if any of them were valuable. Sometimes, I'd pay $1 for a pack of cards and find that one of the cards was worth $10. Other times, I'd spend $1 and find that I only had 50 cents' worth of baseball cards in the whole stack.

No matter how valuable or worthless the *Beckett Price Guide* said my cards were, I could always trade up for some of my buddies' cards. Inevitably, I could trade a card worth 50 cents for a buddy's card that was worth a dollar. My friends had the same pricing guide I had, yet at times they were willing to trade their more valuable cards for my less valuable cards. Why? Did the *Beckett Price Guide* wrongly undervalue my card? Or did my buddy just overpay?

The Mystery of Value

When you deal in the world of values, you will find that a purchase price can often be higher or lower than a guideline. Discrepancies like that happen in real estate, the car industry, collectible trading, and any other industries that offer commodities for sale.

To understand the mystery of value, you have to look at its various types. People say they want to pay market value or fair market value for a product, but is market value accurate? You see, there are several different types of value, and each type has its own price point. So, ultimately, if you're trying to increase value, you have to understand which type of value you need to increase. Which *type* of value determines the price of your shares?

The Various Types of Value in Business

1. Fair market value

First, your business has a fair market value (FMV). At its most basic level, FMV is the price at which a property, business, or asset would sell on the open market. It's the price that a willing, reasonably knowledgeable buyer and seller would agree upon. Both buyer and seller are familiar with pricing guidelines and market variances, and both agree that the asset is worth X amount of dollars.

Most often, FMV is assigned to a business or its assets for tax purposes. *IRS Revenue Ruling 59-60* governs FMV and determines a business's worth in order to assess its personal and property taxes.[8] FMV can also be used to determine a business's value in circumstances where business partners or spouses are separating or divorcing and need to divide equity.

2. Fair value

Next, your business has a fair value. Fair value is not too different from FMV. It is similar in that it's the price that willing buyers and willing sellers agree upon. However, its value is often determined by the open market or the securities market (stock market) rather than the IRS. Per IRS guidelines, accountants will often use a discounting method in small businesses to determine the fair value of a piece of equipment. Additionally, accountants or trustees will use fair value to determine the price of 409A employee stock option plans.

3. Market value

Most commonly referred to as the market capitalization rate, market value is determined by the current value of your business's stocks. In a publicly traded company, you can determine market value by multiplying the number of outstanding shares of stock by their current price on the market. For instance, let's say that your company has a hundred thousand shares of stock. Each share is priced at $20. So, take our stock price, one hundred thousand, and multiply it by 20 gives your business a market value of $2 million.

4. Investment value

Investment value is the value of an asset to a particular investor. In your business, you may have someone appraise your company and say that it is worth X amount of dollars on paper. However, a potential buyer might offer you a little bit more money because it's worth more to him or her. The buyer might look at your company and think they could receive a quick return on their investment, so they're willing to take a risk and pay more than the appraiser's valuation.

5. Strategic value

Many times, buyers will own a business totally unrelated to yours. However, they'll make a strategic move to buy your business because it will complement theirs. They see something in your company that could grow their company. Maybe a buyer has a company that fixes water line leaks, and your company repairs roads and resurfaces them. They're willing to pay a little bit more to acquire your company than another buyer would because it will benefit their existing company.

Let's go back to baseball cards. The Atlanta Braves have always been my team because I grew up in Georgia. I wish they had won at least one more World Series during the 1990s outside of 1995, and I wish they'd get back there again. Let's say I have the entire team set of Braves cards from 2000 Topps, but I'm missing one player's card in mint condition: right fielder Brian Jordan, who was a solid player for the Braves (like Deion Sanders, Jordan also played in the NFL). That's the only card I'm missing, and my friend has that card and wants to trade. I might be willing to trade $1.50 or $2 worth of cards to get a card that's worth 50 cents because it has strategic value. There's synergy between the Brian Jordan card and the rest of the Braves set.

6. Book value

The book value of your business is simply what the balance sheet says your company is worth. Although this seems relatively simple, I caution you about using it to value your company. You see, many business owners depreciate their assets and equipment in their books as a write-off against their income taxes. Therefore, their companies' balance sheets likely indicate that their assets are relatively worthless. The book value may also fail to reflect recent trends.

For example, you may have just invested a significant portion of funds into research and development, which has not yet yielded revenue that would reflect on your income statement. Therefore, the balance sheet would capture the potential asset but not the increase in net operating income.

7. Liquidation value

This is what you can sell your technologies and equipment for if you're trying to close your company. It's the maximum price people will pay for your assets as a result of the dissolution. This value is often substantially less than what is desired by an owner.

8. Forced liquidation value

In a forced liquidation, investors or banks are typically closing your company because you cannot pay your liens. In an attempt to recoup their losses, investors will set a sales date and time to auction off your assets for the maximum amount sale attendees will pay. This method of disposition often results in the lowest return for the business owner.

9. Collateral value

Your business could also have what's called a collateral value. Put simply, collateral value is the amount of money a lender is willing to lend you against the assets you have within your organization.

The Most Important Type of Business Value

Ultimately, you can determine the worth of your business using any of the types of value listed above. And when people talk about the value of your company, they could be talking about any of those values.

However, you can't directly increase or decrease any of the above values. You aren't in control of markets, securities, or lenders. You can't predict economic, political, or environmental changes. Therefore, if you're trying to grow the value of your business, another type of value must exist.

When I talk about growing the value of your business, I'm refer-

ring to the only type of value you can affect—your business's *intrinsic value*, which is determined through a fundamental analysis of your business's quantitative and qualitative factors.

Intrinsic value is a holistic look at your business's capital, earnings, revenue, and profits (the quantitative) along with its management, culture, intellectual capital, and more (the qualitative). You can work to increase the quantitative and qualitative factors. You can take action to increase your income and decrease your expenses. You can hire fantastic team members and create a culture of kindness. You can make business plans, marketing plans, and exit plans that revitalize your company and increase its influence within your marketplace.

Yes, you can use these types of strategies and many more to affect your company's intrinsic value. And if you drive up the intrinsic value of your business, you can drive up all the other values listed above.

Business Valuation (and How It Works)

It's one thing for me to tell you that you should increase your business's intrinsic value to attract customers, investors, or buyers. It's another thing for me to tell you *how* to increase it. Before I can do that, you need to understand how business valuation works from an appraiser's perspective.

Price or Value?

If business owners are seeking investors or buyers, they're often concerned about the price others will pay them for their business or equity in their business. **Although buyers and investors care about the price they will pay for a business, they're more concerned about the *value* they will get for their investment.**

Let's say my mom wants to buy a new car because her current car is getting old. She wants a brand-new car because she's never had one before. She usually buys used cars and drives them until the wheels fall off (literally). In her quest, she starts by looking at styles, colors, and features. She is trying to weigh luxury against practicality. As she visits car lots, the salespeople highlight the value each type of vehicle could bring to her life.

Ultimately, the price of the vehicle comes up, and she'll likely determine that the price is more important than value. Conversely, when it comes to business, the seller is often more focused on the price than the buyer.

The **seller** tries to highlight transactional value to convince a buyer to write a check and sign their name. Maybe the seller will highlight the conditions of the economy, market, or industry.

Those looking at your business from the outside will ask a lot of questions. They might ask: Is this business viable? Does it offer quality goods and services? Does the business have transferable patents, copyrights, or trademarks? Is the business centered around one good customer, or does it have multiple customers? Are the customers loyal? What about the team members and managers? Are they older or younger? Will they be around a long time? Are they overpaid or underpaid? Are there up-to-date operational systems in place, and are they utilized appropriately?

All those questions center around value. So, which is more important to buyers and investors? Warren Buffet once said, "Price is what you pay. Value is what you get."[9] If you're looking at your business from a buyer's perspective, then you want to build a business so valuable that buyers are willing to pay a higher price than the market says your business is worth.

Three Business Valuation Approaches

Now that you understand the concept of value compared to price and *value compared to profitability*, you need to know how appraisers determine your business's value. Suppose you strip business valuation down to its most basic level. In that case, you'll see that appraisers tend to use one of three approaches to determine your business's worth: the market approach, the asset approach, or the income approach. Among the three, one is king. But you need to understand all of them to understand how to grow value in your own company.

1. The market approach

The key to this approach relates to whether your company is publicly traded or privately held.

The Guideline Public Company Method

If your company is large and publicly traded, then appraisers will look at the prices that comparable companies' shares have sold for on the Dow, the S&P 500, or the Russell 2000 to determine your shares' value. This is called the **guideline public company method**. Although this approach works really well for large, publicly traded companies, it's hard to compare a company of that size to a midsize or small private company. Therefore, you will not likely be affected by this method.

The Guideline M&A Transaction Method

Appraisers are more likely to use the **guideline M&A transaction method** to determine the value of your small or midsize business. Here, evaluators look at the sales of companies similar to yours within your industry. They narrow down your industry based on your business's classification within the North American industry classification system (NAICS) or within the standard industrial classification code (SIC). Then business appraisers will assess how similar the sold businesses within your industry are to yours. Are they in the same location? Do you serve similar customers? Is their revenue stream comparable to yours?

Unfortunately, most private companies' information is, well, ... *private*. Therefore, appraisers often have a difficult time comparing your company to other private companies due to not having access to the other companies' revenue streams, profit margins, or demographics. The lack of public information makes determining your business's worth extremely difficult in a market approach method.

2. The asset approach

To avoid the difficulty of a market approach, many business appraisers will use an asset approach to determine a company's value. They'll review your company's financial records and run necessary calculations to determine the value of your tangible or intangible assets.

The Adjusted Net Asset Value

First, appraisers can calculate your company's adjusted net asset value. Although this technique sounds intimidating, it's relatively straightforward. Essentially, it's the replacement value of your assets and liabilities in the event of a disaster or a sale. It could be the calculated value of your assets if you lose everything in a fire, or it could be the amount of money you'd get for your assets if you were to sell them.

To determine this replacement or liquidation value, appraisers look at your company's balance sheet. They see how much your assets are worth on paper. Then, they subtract any liabilities you owe on the assets. Because this method uses your company's book valuation of your assets, it's often used as the baseline, or floor, method of your company. If you've depreciated your assets on paper, be wary of having an appraiser use this method to determine your business's value.

Excess Earnings Method

Another asset appraisal approach is called the excess earnings method. It's more complicated than the adjusted net asset value method but basically involves an evaluator determining intangible assets' value. Since this particular calculation method assesses things like revenue from a blog or royalty income from published works, it's very seldom used to determine a company's worth in the event of a sale.

3. The income approach

If appraisers typically don't use the market approach or the asset approach to determine a company's value, what do they use? Well, here's the important part. Whenever it comes time for you to have your business appraised for sale or investment purposes, an evaluator will usually look at your income or your cash flow and compare it to the risks your business faces. In fact, the income approach is so valuable that Shannon P. Pratt, the chairman of Shannon Pratt Valuations, writes about it in his book, *Valuing a Business: The Analysis and Appraisal of Closely Held Companies*. He says, "The income approach is king. Hands down. The income approach is key. Whatever approaches to value are used, they should be reconciled with the income approach."[10]

Capitalized Historical Cash Flow Method

Within the income approach, you'll find the capitalized historical cash flow method. Just like it sounds, this appraisal approach looks at your historical cash flow. The appraiser takes the weighted average of that cash flow and divides it by a capitalization rate, or cap rate, which reflects your business's risk factors and its expected growth in the future.

The downside to using this cash flow method is that appraisers must use their judgment to develop a capitalization rate. They determine the specific risks companies have and how much those risk factors affect the companies. Therefore, the cap rate can vary from appraiser to appraiser, which means your value can differ from one appraiser to another appraiser.

Discounted Future Cash Flow Method

Appraisers who use the discounted future cash flow method value project future cash flows of your company and then discount the future cash flow with a discount rate that reflects the riskiness of the future cash flow. Obviously, I'm trying to simplify the process. Essentially, they're discounting your business's value according to the riskiness of the future cash flow.

The tricky part of the discounted future cash flow method is that appraisers have to make a subjective decision about when your company's cash flow will cease, reduce, grow, etc. Your business will not last forever. Therefore, appraisers must make an educated guess as to when your company's cash flow will cease or terminate.

Why Business Valuation Matters

I'm not telling you that you need to learn how to value your company, but you need to understand the various approaches to business valuation. Cash is king—or, in the world of valuation, **the income approach is king**. And within the income approach, appraisers either look backward to see what your company has done, or they look forward to see what your company has the potential to do. Profits alone don't determine your company's historical growth, nor do they determine your future potential. Your company's qualitative factors increase or decrease the quantitative numbers that appraisers use to value your business. Your qualitative and quantitative factors together increase the overall value of your company.

You have to understand the rules of the game. Imagine trying to play football or baseball without knowing the rules—you'd never win. What makes you think you can grow your company's value to the point you can sell it for profit if you don't know the rules appraisers are using to value it? Now that you have more of an idea, it's time to find out which qualitative factors drive up your business's perceptible factors.

Intrinsic Value and Pizza Slices

Having a profitable business with consistent and predictable cash flow is important to your company's survival. However, if cash flow, revenue, and profits—the quantitative sides of your business—are the only things you seek to improve, then the qualitative sides of your business will suffer. Although it's easy to identify your business's quantitative factors, it's harder to identify its qualitative factors. For that reason, I want to identify eight foundational components that drive up your business's intrinsic value, otherwise known as its qualitative worth.

The easiest way for me to illustrate the eight components that drive up your business's qualitative worth is to place them on a pie chart, like slices of a pizza pie. (Just don't put any pineapple on my slice!)

1. Planning

If you're trying to increase your business's intrinsic value, you must start with planning. Planning is often one of the weakest areas of your business, yet it is fundamental to growth. If you don't plan, then you have no direction, nowhere to go, and no way to get there. How can you make improvements if you don't identify and determine ways to capitalize on your company's strengths and improve its weaknesses?

8 KEY AREAS OF BUSINESS

- PLANNING
- LEADERSHIP
- FINANCE
- LEGAL
- SALES
- MARKETING
- PEOPLE
- OPERATIONS

2. Leadership

The second slice of your pizza pie is leadership, which can be found throughout your entire organization. To increase your business's intrinsic value, you must build leadership from both the top down and the bottom up.

3. Sales

Next, you come to your business's sales division. To grow your qualitative worth, you not only have to sell, but you need to have a sales *process*. You must specify the verbiage you want to use and the types of customers you want to reach, among other things.

4. Marketing

Although marketing complements your sales department, most business owners neglect it as much as they do planning. To increase your business's value, you cannot advertise anywhere, everywhere, or nowhere. You must develop a marketing plan that gets your company's message to the right people.

5. People

Now let's look at your team members. Do you have them positioned properly within your company? Do their personalities match their skill sets? Are you communicating your business's culture and values to them effectively? Are your people prepared for any type of shift or transition that may take place as a result of your exit?

6. Operations

If you have people within your organization, you must have operational structures and systems. Are you using the right ones? And are you utilizing them efficiently?

7. Finance

Most small-business owners think that because their CPA or tax advisor handles their books, they don't have to worry about their business finances. This couldn't be further from the truth. Finance goes through the heart of your company. It shows you how to quantify what you're trying to achieve, so it's just as valuable as the other slices in your pizza pie.

8. Legal

Finally, you must work to strengthen and improve the legal aspects of your business in order to grow your company's intrinsic value. Here, you're making sure that you're compliant with laws, contracts, and agreements. It's shoring your business up against worst-case scenarios so that you and your business are protected from harm.

Personality Profiles within Your Business's Fundamental Components

Within your company's eight foundational components, you have four core areas:

- Planning and leadership
- Sales and marketing
- Operations and people
- Finance and legal

If you overlay a personality assessment tool (I prefer DiSC, because it's familiar and straightforward, but there are other popular assessments like the Myers-Briggs Type Indicator) on each of these sections, you'll notice something interesting.

Dominant and Influential Personalities

The people in your planning and leadership departments tend to have *D*, or **dominant**, personalities. They are decisive, driven, results-oriented people, often your CEOs. The people in your sales and marketing team tend to land in the *I* quadrant and have **influential** personalities. These interactive, optimistic, fun, social people are best used within your company to engage customers and clients.

Steady and Compliant Personalities

Next, you have *S* personalities, your **steady** supporters, overseeing your

DISC PERSONALITIES

D - DOMINATE   S - STEADY

I - INFLUENCE   C - COMPLIANT

PLANNING   SALES

LEADERSHIP   MARKETING

FINANCE   PEOPLE

LEGAL   OPERATIONS

operations and people. They approach tasks systematically and work in assisting roles within your company. Finally, your finance and legal people tend to have *C*, or **compliant**, personalities. They are analytical and accurate and fuss over minute details and numbers instead of getting involved in drama or chaos within your organization.

If you apply the DiSC assessment personality model to your business's four fundamental components, you have a powerful device. You can identify your team members' personality strengths and then place them in roles that will strengthen each of your organization's core areas. By doing that, you can begin growing the qualitative value of your business.

The Bottom Line

We know statistically that the average business doesn't sell. It's not because of a lack of profit. It's due to a lack of strategically preparing the business for sale. We have to look at value through an investor's eyes.

Just because your friend, sister, or your cousin sold their business for X doesn't mean you will. It's what's actually under the hood of the business that determines its value. I remember years ago watching a street race where two Chevy Camaros pulled up to the line. One Camaro was stock and had a typical V-8 engine. The other one had a souped-up engine, and the internal and external changes made the car fast and powerful. When you looked at the two cars, they looked and sounded the same. But when the light turned green and they began racing down the drag road, the car that had the high-performance engine, rear end, tires, and transmission accelerated past the stock vehicle.

Looks can be deceiving! Value comes through the ways you soup up your company.

WHAT

CHAPTER 2

Planning: Why Your Baby Is Ugly

I f you're trying to increase your business's intrinsic value, you must start with **planning**. Planning is often a weak area, yet it's fundamental to growing a business and ultimately making it sellable. If you don't plan, you have no direction, nowhere to go, and no way to get there. How can you make improvements if you don't identify your company's strengths and weaknesses?

Entrepreneurs are passionate, driven, and courageous by nature. As I often say, they're willing to charge hell with a water pistol. But what happens when they get there? Will they even get there? What's the plan?

Many small-business owners are poor long-term planners. As the old saying goes, fail to plan, and you plan to fail. We're used to planning in our everyday lives. We make a plan of the route we'll drive from one town to the next. We plan what we're going to eat for dinner tonight. (I hope it's a New York–style thin-crust, meat-lovers pizza—sorry, Chicago!)

But long-term planning is tougher to grasp. Business owners are often so consumed by daily business operations that they don't take time to plan for the future, inevitably leading to setbacks that keep them in the hamster wheel of day-to-day worries. **It doesn't need to be that way.**

Planning for the Future

Charles Schwab surveyed 1,000 people actively saving for retirement, and more than half said they spent five hours doing research the last time they bought a car.[11] That's a lot of time! And 39 percent said they spent more than five hours looking at vacation possibilities. My wife loves to pick out places for us to go—I bet she spends more than five hours planning our vacations.

Here's where it gets interesting: only 11 percent of the people surveyed said they spent that same amount of time analyzing or evaluating their retirement plans. In fact, only about one-third of savers said they spent at least an hour on any type of research. From my experience, I have to believe that we business owners would score even lower.

We spend more time planning our cars and vacations than we do planning our retirement, but before we pick on the lack of retirement planning too much, let's talk about us business owners. The Alternative Board, also known as TAB, published a Business Pulse Survey that showed 73 percent of business owners would prefer to work less in their business. I get that, and I want to work less in my business too. Notably, about 40 percent of the study's participants admitted to having an ineffective or nonexistent operating plan and budget.[12]

The TAB Business Pulse Survey went on to show that less than 30 percent work *on* their business; most spend the bulk of their time working *in* their business. I know that in my businesses I've made every excuse under the sun about why I can put planning off until later. I'm no exception, and I've seen the consequences of failing to plan.

Let's take it a step further: according to the Exit Planning Institute's State of the Markets Study, only about 25 percent of business owners even have a basic written personal financial plan.[13] If business owners are not willing to prepare for their personal financial future, how well will they plan for the future of the business, which can be much more complicated? Often, we business owners (myself included) are too busy to stop and put the time into planning our future moves.

Army General and President Dwight D. Eisenhower said, regarding going into battle, "I've always found that plans are useless, but planning is essential."[14] I'm usually drawn to the first part of that statement: plans change. But what about the second part: planning is essential?

During my training, I learned that planning consistently lags behind other areas of business in terms of how important it is considered by business owners. So, **planning** ranks lower than **leadership, sales, marketing, people, operations, finance**, and **legal**, yet planning is the first area I will focus on here. It is first for a good reason. Planning is widely misunderstood. Entrepreneur, influencer, John Lee Dumas says it well: "A good plan now is better than a great plan later." Devote your attention to proper planning, and it could transform your company.

What Is Business Planning?

Knowing that most business owners fail to realize the importance of planning or fail to plan correctly (or at all), it's essential that we look at what exactly *is* business planning.

> **Business planning is a fundamental management function involving the design, steps, and quantification needed to achieve an optimum balance of needs or demands with available resources.**

Ultimately, the definition of business planning can be understood by working through the business-planning process. Whether you're planning your business's opening, growth, projects, risk mitigation, sale, closing, or anything else, **all planning begins with a process**. Although you can make the planning process as long or as complicated as you like, I tend to break it down into four basic steps.

- **Step 1: Decide what you're going to do.**
  Identify goals or objectives to be achieved.

- **Step 2: Determine how you will do it.**
  Formulate strategies to achieve the goals or objectives.

- **Step 3: Pick who will accomplish it.**
  Arrange the people required to enact the strategies and work toward the goals.

- **Step 4: Take action.**
  Implement, direct, and monitor the steps of the action plan.

What Is the Exact Status of Your Company Today, and Why Is It There?

I see so many business owners who don't have a clear understanding of their company's status. I use "status" here, rather than "health," "finances," or any other word because a company is a very fluid beast. I've had to send prospective clients back to their offices to do research because they have no clue of their companies' current health. They bring in profit and loss statements (P&L), and they show me financial data. I have to tell them, "No, let's dig down to the numbers that are driving these points."

When you're doing a company's assessment for planning, you're going to have to ask the tough questions—for example,

- Why are we doing what we're doing?
- Why are we at this point?
- What good or bad choices did we make to bring us to this present position?
- Should we stop or add elements to our business?
- What are the projects on the horizon? When are they expected to begin and end?
- How do we measure success?
- What does it mean to win?

BUSINESS PLANNING

1. STEP #1

Decide what you are going to do.

Identify goals or objectives to be achieved.

2. STEP #2

Determine how you will do it.

Formulate strategies to achieve the goals or objectives.

3. STEP #3

Pick who will accomplish it.

Arrange the people required to enact the strategies and work toward the goals.

4. STEP #4

Take action.

Implement, direct, and monitor the steps of the action plan.

- Where do the planned activities take place?

I often use an example of traveling from Knoxville, Tennessee, to Portland, Oregon. Those two cities are separated by about 2,500 miles.

Is the "action" going to take place in a car, train, or plane? What are the various steps of the trip? Before I get in the car and hit the gas pedal, I have to know many important details. Which route am I going to drive? Do I want to take my time and see the sights, or do I want to burn rubber? Will I stop and eat, or will I pack a lunch? Where am I going to stay when I arrive in Portland? How long am I going to be there? What am I going to do when I arrive? Now you realize how many essential details must be addressed before I embark on my journey.

Business planning is not much different. We must know the details of our plan to prepare for the trip properly and what resources will be needed to make the plan successful. These are just some of the questions that need to be answered in a detailed planning process. All business plans outline the actions business owners, managers, and employees must take to make a business successful.

Before you begin the planning process, you must include the following items:

- lists of who is involved in the planning process
- an assessment of your business's current strengths and weaknesses
- the reasoning behind your plans
- project start and end dates
- measurements you will use to determine the success or failure of your plans
- areas or departments in which you will take action
- ways in which you will take action
- a list of resources you will need to take action
- what contingencies you will encounter along the way

Compiling all of those details is *tedious* work. Business planning can be frustrating and challenging, and it can cause short-term disruptions to business operations. When you're doing any type of business planning,

you're going to evaluate your business, your baby, and realize that it's ugly. Your love usually only lets you see the good in your baby, and that means you miss some important things—the things that are going to hold your business back from reaching its potential. You're going to need to change some things about your baby. You're also going to need to change how you view your baby.

It's hard. But just because something is hard, it doesn't mean it's bad. And just because something is tedious, it doesn't mean you shouldn't do it. Struggle can be beneficial. A butterfly must go through the struggle of breaking out of its chrysalis to gain the strength to fly. The same can be true of your business. These planning details are good for you, for your team, and for your business.

Remember, **to affect the future, you must disrupt the present.** You have to create some turmoil to improve. Think about a rocket ship. For a rocket ship to go upward into orbit, it must have combustion—disruption. Planning disrupts business because it makes you stop and think about what you're doing well or poorly. Planning gives you a chance to improve and fix your company's weak points.

Why Business Planning Matters, and Why It's So Difficult

A business plan helps you identify where you've been and decide where you're going. It covers the company's history and helps set a path for every new and current employee to follow. Additionally, a business plan is going to identify your target customer and market concentration. It's going to document your company's mission and vision, your objectives, and ultimately, your strategies.

Whereas **vision** is more aspirational and involves the private aims you discuss within your company, the **mission** is inspirational—it's your company's story that you share with the community at large. And as you decide on your vision and mission, planning will force you to define your company's values. **Values** are a reflection of your standards as a business owner. What is your driving force? What do you stand for? What will you compromise on? What *won't* you compromise on?

Planning will also help you dive into your company's strengths, its impacts on customers, how it aligns in comparison with your competition, as well as how it should be structured. Frequently, owners will think that because they have managers, key players, or department heads, they have done planning—planning through delegation or obfuscation. However, leadership must take diligent approaches to move a company forward and plan its actions.

But here's the hard part and the reason why planning is a technique that's so underused with business owners: You can't properly create a business plan until you've addressed the other seven areas of the process. You can't have a business plan until you create a sales and marketing plan. You can't have a business plan until you know your limitations involving risk management or legal issues. A business plan requires all the other areas of the business so that strategy can be implemented throughout.

Planning comes first because each of the other areas rely on its fundamentals. The process comes full circle after you have developed the other areas and allows you to create a robust business plan. It's going to improve and be influenced by the other foundational components that drive up your company's value.

Missing Your Turn

Often when I talk about planning with business owners, there's a significant disconnect regarding how planning affects day-to-day operations. Many business owners are so focused on the immediate that they forget about the future. It reminds me of my drive to work. I drive about 20 miles to work every day: down country roads, along the interstate, and through the Tennessee mountains. I see deer and turkey just about every morning on my drive.

I like that drive—it gives me a chance to clear my head. On Sundays, when I go to church, my habit is to use the same route I take to the office, and then my wife has to remind me, "You just missed the exit again." Because I'm so focused on my routine, I end up taking the wrong turn because it's familiar, even though it's not where I'm going.

Let's compare the world of planning to driving a car. Many of us are so focused on the road in front of us and what's around the next corner that we forget where we want to be headed. Business owners are often so focused on the next step that they're not thinking about where they're going to end up. As the old saying goes, if you aim at nothing, you're going to hit it every time.

Growth over Profits

Far too often, business owners chase profits, believing this to be the best method of increasing their business value. However, this is a misconception that will leave you exhausted and disappointed more often than not. This is because you are not decreasing company-specific risk (CSR)—risk that only applies to your specific company. You are often forsaking the company's critical systems by chasing profits, which will prove shortsighted when it comes time to sell. Growing activity, revenue, or profits does not equal growing value, and CSR is the key. Reduce the CSR and increase the value.

At this point, you might be thinking, "Dude, there's no way. I'm doing all I can just to keep my sanity!" I get it! That's why you end up hiring someone like me, someone who can look holistically at your company and challenge you. This is why coaches exist—in business, sports, and life. You need somebody who is in your corner and can walk you through the steps necessary for improvement.

Recently, I held a two-day planning session with a company. The business owner told me, "Justin, I want to sell the business in five years."

"Cool, let's make it happen," I said. "But we've got to double the value of the business for you to reach your personal financial goals in the five-year time frame."

"Good luck with that," he responded.

"No, it's not luck. We're going to develop a plan, quantify the data, and get to work," I said.

We flew to a different state for the meeting, which was effective because we could get the key decision makers on board with the objectives before bringing in their 17 employees to focus on strategies, tactics, and actions.

Why did we bring the employees into the conversation? Because it's best to get feedback from the whole organization. A study says that leaders of the company only know about 4 percent of the organization's problems. The concept is called the "iceberg of ignorance" and was popularized by consultant Sidney Yoshida in 1989.[15]

I was in a meeting not too long ago with a sizable service-based company, and the business owner said, "When I was relying on just my management team for recommendations, I was missing so much information from the people in the battle. But once I started getting recommendations from my frontline employees, I started to get a much better perspective on what was going on and what parts of the company needed attention."

It's like if an army goes to war and the troops on the ground try to call in support, but the people back at the office who aren't fighting keep second-guessing everything. You lose soldiers, lose internal support in the mission, and don't secure victory in the battle.

How Planning Brings Value

The following sample value-maximization process questions can help you gauge your company's planning efforts and define areas of focus to help you achieve greater value.

Business Roadmap

- Does your company have a documented and encyclopedic business plan?
- Is your senior management team involved in your business planning?
- Is there an independent dream team of consultants involved in this business plan (CPA*, Attorney, Certified Financial Planner®)?

First of all, you want to find out if a written business plan exists and if it's fully developed. Meaning, if a written plan exists, have all the business owners, developers, employees, and management contributed to the document and established a system that can track the business's successes and struggles?

You want to see if the plan has been updated. If it hasn't, then often the business owner is just riding by the seat of their pants. They're running around fixing immediate problems, but there's a new one every day. What we want to see is that the business owner is working through a plan to a purpose.

Does this mean a buyer's going to be asking for a business plan? Maybe, maybe not, but by looking at the business plan and its outcomes, they'll be able to tell if the company is in survival mode or if it's strategically planning to increase the company's value. A business plan shows us that the company is strategically moving toward a goal and not just flailing like a fish out of water.

Even though it seems like a mundane task, draft the skeleton of your business plan, and begin working on completing it. Download a sample business plan worksheet at financiallysimple.com/otc-strategic-planning-worksheet/.

The Perfect Customer

- Have you identified a specific target client or customer?
- What region is being targeted?
- Is demand in the market growing or contracting?

It's not uncommon for business owners who enter business with a good product or service to lose sight of their targeted market over time. They lose the image of the "perfect customer," whoever that may be. Many business owners also fail to recognize if market demand is growing or contracting. Imagine trying to put up a DVD or a CD rental store right now. It would be illogical!

Years ago, I worked with a client whose customer was the US government. All they did was make products for the US military—that was their *only* customer. And it wasn't even the whole military; it was just one branch. And it was one particular widget and that widget only. Having such a limited customer base will reduce the value of the company. We have to identify the current target market and make sure that it is established and has a growing demand.

My company's target market is business owners who are typically between the ages of 35 and 60 years old. They're not usually new business owners, as they have some miles behind them. They've heard the sales pitches and seen the fly-by-night business consultants come and go.

They've dealt with newbie financial advisors or business consultants who want to try to sell them some product or service. That's not what they're after—they need someone to work alongside them and help them reach their goals. We know that our target market needs somebody who will fill the chair across from them and understand their lonely position and what keeps them up at night. So, we're the first people they call, not a CPA or attorney. They can contact us with any type of question.

That is who we serve. That is who we pour our precious time and talents into. Typically family-oriented, our average Frazzled Frank or Franny is married and middle to upper-middle class. We're not dealing with the überaffluent, nor are we dealing with people who are broke. That's not who our Frazzled Frank or Franny is. We have an actual living, breathing person in mind. We know where they like to shop and their favorite foods. (They better like pizza.) They're people I wouldn't mind sitting in a tree stand with for a week at a time, or going climbing in the backcountry, or sharing a fishing boat.

Competitors

- Does the company have direct challengers or competition? If so, do they offer specific threats or risks to the company?
- Is there pressure on billing rates as technology evolves?
- What share does the company have in its target market?

It's natural to face direct competition, and it's important to understand it. If you watch *Shark Tank* regularly, you'll often see somebody pitching a little doodad that a bigger firm could easily steal and then crush the smaller company's growth plan. Companies today face a wider range of threats than ever before, including online shopping and mobile services. Understanding your competition will help you better understand your own company.

Some further questions to ask yourself include the following:

- Who are your top three competitors?
- Why are they viewed as competition?
- What are they doing well, and where can you disrupt their business?
- What do you see that you like?
- How's their marketing?
- If you were to analyze their business as a purchaser, what would you say?
- Where are their strengths?
- Where are their weaknesses?

Businesses are getting pressure from a revenue standpoint, a margin standpoint, from billing rates and fee rates, so they're price sensitive. It's almost like a race to the bottom in many areas, but doing that is not going to drive up your company's value.

When I think of competition, I often think of this story: an old-school barber, the type with the spinning candy cane pole outside of his shop, is well established and gives good haircuts. There isn't much competition in the area until a chain salon comes in across the street. This chain places a big sign outside and one of those dancing men attached to a fan, which catches drivers' attention. The sign reads "We give $6 haircuts." As time goes on, the barber notices a decrease in revenue. His haircuts cost $27, and he hasn't raised his price in years and feels he earns what he charges. So, he takes action and adds his own sign out front that says "I fix $6 haircuts."

He does not lower his price—he voices his value. And his plan works! He is able to stabilize his business, and it begins growing again. If you have a business model that knows its competition, doesn't focus on undercutting them with pricing, doesn't have too much competition to begin with, and is disrupting the marketplace, then you've got a clear path forward to adding value for potential buyers.

Obstructions to Market Entry

- Are there obstacles, or can any company enter your company's industry?
- Is there a need for skilled human capital to readily compete in the market?
- How do reputation or regulations restrict entry into the industry?

I think of my first business, the landscape business I owned when I was 16 years old. We could go out and earn business away from established companies. Some guy in a truck could go and take away a very sizable account from a well-established, prominent business in town. There was a low barrier to entry, which weakens a business's value.

Suppose there is a high barrier to entry, such as a license, a credential, a knowledge level, or board certification. In that case, it's going to increase the value of a company because fewer other businesses will be able to enter the industry. A sophisticated IT company could provide an integration platform used by engineers working on a special project. It would involve numerous regulations and well-trained employees, and it's not something just anyone could do. As such, this high barrier to entry would yield a higher business value.

Industry Growth

- Do technological innovations or advancements often disrupt the industry?
- Does your company focus on creating innovative products and services within your marketplace?
- Are there efforts to penetrate new segments of the industry?
- Is your company trying to uncover new thought leadership within the marketplace?

If your business is vulnerable to technological changes—in other words, if somebody could come along and create a new technology that could drastically disrupt your business—then you could lose value in your company. But if you're the ones who are constantly on the cutting edge, trying to drive the value of your company through new technological advancements, then you up the odds of increasing its value. I love the story of 3M, which was initially known as Minnesota Mining and Manufacturing Company when it was founded in 1902. They're no longer purely a mining company—they've changed and transformed themselves multiple times over the years, and now they make paint, tape, and epoxies.

It's like that famous quote by hockey legend Wayne Gretzky: "Skate to where the puck is going, not where it has been."[16] As a business owner, you need to keep thinking about where the proverbial puck is going in your market. You want to be ahead of trends and in a position to offset any type of disruption. You're always trying to figure out where you're going and how to get there before your competition. Waiting for the puck to come to you or lingering where the puck once was isn't going to help you position your company for success or drive its value.

The Bottom Line

Being able to show that your company is devoted to planning—from its board of directors to its senior management and beyond—is going to make you look so much better to a prospective buyer, and it's going to bring you greater reward for your effort. Planning will bring you a higher multiple inside your business, giving you a higher sale price. With all of these in-depth adjustments, you're inevitably going to drive up the revenue of your business. You're going to keep your expenses down, causing the EBITDA of your business to drastically increase. Planning is vital to driving value because it forces you to look into the future. You're taking time to work on the future health of your business. Most people don't do that.

Action Item: Planning

Close your eyes for a few moments and think about where you want your company to be in three years.

- How successful is the business in terms of revenue?
- What goods or services are you providing?
- Where are you positioned in the market?
- What is your company's structure?

That mental model should guide you as you approach your business plan. As you begin mapping out the journey ahead, it's helpful to have an idea in mind of where you want to wind up.

If you need additional help with your company's business plan or feel like you could benefit from one-on-one coaching, please reach out to me at JustinGoodbread.com.

CHAPTER 3

Leadership: How to Be a Better Parent to Your Baby

The second slice of your pizza pie is **leadership**, which is found throughout your entire organization. To increase your business's intrinsic value, you must build leadership from the **top down** *and* **bottom up**.

Leaders come in many forms and fashions. A leader could be a single person or a group of people in charge of operations, activities, people, or decisions. But putting someone in charge of operations or colleagues doesn't necessarily make them a *good* leader. Is a leader someone who directs a group of people in an organization to accomplish a common goal? Sure. But just standing back and barking orders doesn't make for a good leader. Growing the value of your company requires good leaders and good leadership. But how do you find good leaders or know how to identify good leadership for your company?

The Book on Leadership

Have you ever walked into a bookstore? I know we shop more and more online these days, but I love going into a bookstore and checking out new books, whether it's a local bookstore, independent bookstore, or a chain.

There's a section in our Books-A-Million store in Knoxville that's devoted to leadership. I can see it on the wall. There are always a couple dozen books on leadership that become notable every year. They typically include what I call a mountaintop story, where someone who went through some ordeal is now on top of the mountain, saying, "Hey, look how I did it! Follow me!" Others detail corporate success stories, recounting consultants' past achievements or department heads of companies to try and inspire you to do the same thing they did. Some involve personal tragedies, which I can empathize with. I have dealt with my share of hard times in business, and those hard times left scars.

I don't usually think these books are helpful. Times change, and the things that drove success in the 1990s or early 2000s or even yesterday aren't necessarily going to work tomorrow. I'm not interested in addressing leadership from a mountaintop because I'm not there. When you arrive there, it is often not long before life knocks you off for yet another climb. I don't want to address leadership from a corporate success perspective because I've never been a corporate employee—and Lord, please don't make me air out my struggles.

I rarely see leadership books that aren't limited to narratives about mountaintops or corporate successes or tragedies when they're written for small-business owners *by* small-business owners. I want to address leadership from a small-business owner's mindset because that's who I am. I want to deal specifically with how leadership ties directly to value in a small business.

Leadership, Defined

Dolly Parton is credited with this meaningful quote about leadership: "If your actions create a legacy that inspires others to dream more, learn more, do more, and become more, then, you are an excellent leader."[17] The

Chinese philosopher Lao Tzu also had an important perspective: "A leader is best when people barely know he exists, when his work is done, his aim fulfilled, they will say: we did it ourselves."[18]

The commonality between those quotes is bringing out the best in people. **Leadership isn't a title.** Qualities of a leader are not automatically bestowed on someone just because they're in charge.

You could say leadership is the act of inspiring subordinates to a common mission. There are so many definitions of leadership that fall short. Here's how I define it: **leadership is a person or group of people who set the vision and mission for success through authority, responsibility, ability, strategy, creativity, and decisive actions. They motivate everyone to reach their unknown potential through taking individual responsibility.**

I know it's a mouthful. In simpler terms, and to borrow the Army's former recruiting slogan: leadership is helping others to "be all they can be."[19]

Qualities of Leaders

These are the qualities I believe good leaders should possess if they want to increase the value of a small business:

- Charisma
- Innovation
- Capability
- Responsibility
- Respect
- Strategy
- Vision

Levels of Leadership

Who, then, are the leaders within your small business? Are they the owners, the chief executive officers, the members of the board of directors, or the managers? Yes, but leaders don't always carry fancy titles or badges. Leadership doesn't always flow down from the top; sometimes, rank-and-file employees lead from the bottom up.

In fact, Jim Collins, author of *Good to Great*, claims that leadership is multidirectional in a small-business setting. He says, "We found that for leaders to make something great, their ambition has to be for the greatness of the work and the company rather than for themselves."[20] In other words, he believes that people who work for the good of the company rather than for their own good are leaders within the business no matter their titles or positions. He believes leaders appear in five different levels of a business.

Level I Leaders

First, Collins says that individuals in entry-level positions are leaders if they contribute to the company with their talents, knowledge, skills, and work habits. If you're hiring correctly, your employees are often competent, even at the lower levels.

Level II Leaders

To become a Level II leader, individuals must progress beyond their desire for self-promotion and self-focus to a place where they seek to accomplish something greater than themselves within the company. These leaders acknowledge and pursue group objectives; they're contributing individual capabilities to achieving a more significant cause.

Level III Leaders

Once you pass Level II leadership, recognized leaders can become strong managers or individuals who organize people and resources toward the effective and efficient pursuit of a predetermined objective.

Level IV Leaders

After becoming managers, leaders can become key managers or managers of other leaders. These individuals show a commitment to the pursuit of the company's vision, and they inspire others to reach their full potential to pursue that vision too.

Level V Leaders

Finally, individuals can become executive leaders within the business. These are not the people who start the business and become leaders in name only. These are the people who have walked through leadership levels to prove their effective leadership skills and prove their commitment to the company as a whole. Level V leaders can articulate clear and compelling visions and inspire others to work toward those visions as hard as they do.

Step Back and Step Up

The most effective measure of leadership is the team's performance in your absence, and that's applicable not only in business but in everything that requires teamwork. If you, the business owner, can leave for a period of time and the business can continue forward on an accelerated or climbing trajectory, then your leadership is effective. Your employees are prepared to step up. If you can achieve this level of business efficiency through leadership, you have drastically beautified your baby!

I consulted with a business owner a few years ago who was trying to prepare his business to sell. One of the things I asked him to do was schedule a long hiatus, a sabbatical, where he could leave the organization for three or four weeks during the year's peak without checking in. When I first recommended that, he thought I had lost my ever-loving mind. "If I do that at this time of year, it could make or break my business," he told me.

I understand that he was voicing fear, but he also expressed discomfort with his leadership abilities. So, we decided when his hiatus should take place, we made the team aware, and then we spent the next nine months working toward that event. Lo and behold, the time came, and I didn't think he was going to do it, but he left. He turned off his phone, didn't check his email, and he and his lovely bride traveled for three weeks. The team kept operating in his absence, and … **the business grew**. They had more clients than when the owner had left. Sales were up. Everything was in even better shape. His company's growth while he traveled was a testament to the positive leadership changes he had made.

Get the Right People on the Bus

It starts at the very beginning, and that is with hiring the right people. Jim Collins writes in *Good to Great*, "Get the right people on the bus and then put them in the right seats."[21] We have to hire right, but too often we deal with the "right now," filling the job with the most comfortable available option. Or we misjudge someone's character or fail to do due diligence during the hiring process. Whenever you're building leaders in your organization, you have to make sure you hire the right people from the very beginning.

The old saying goes, hire slow, fire fast, but I found that you don't have to fire fast if you spend time hiring right. To build leaders, **you have to hire people who want to be leaders**. You have to hire the people who desire to participate in the vision. That's number one. Number two is that **you have to have a high standard for leadership**. Suppose someone's position or title in the company infers leadership. The standard of leadership for this individual must exceed that of the workers in an entry-level position. As the old saying goes, to whom much is given, much is required.

Cross-Training Isn't Only about Fitness

You have to set high standards. Some organizations require a certain amount of production. Others require acumen, extensive time commitments, and dedication. However you measure success in your particular business, your leaders have to have a high standard. Here are some ways to raise the standards of your leaders:

- Get everyone in alignment. Your company's leaders have to be able to articulate a crystal clear vision, and the business owner, individual leaders, and the company as a whole must share that vision.
- Include your emerging leaders in your organization's leadership process. You must keep your leaders engaged in the strategic-planning process. The goal is to come out of each leadership meeting able to disseminate the information across all channels. If you're building leaders, have them in your strategic-planning meetings.
- Your leaders need to know about more than just their roles. They

need to understand the company from multiple vantage points, and they need to be able to see things the way their subordinates do.

- Hammer home the goals, mission, and vision. They say repetition is fundamental to learning. If you're training leaders, you must repeat yourself continually. That repetition will put smart actions into practice and prevent bad habits from forming.

- Ask for and implement input. Employees want to know their opinions are valued. Engaging in open dialogue and encouraging feedback will help you recognize potential leaders while sharpening your business operations.

- Some of us are downright lousy leaders. Find those who aren't. I often consult with business owners who have team members who are better leaders than the owner. I strongly encourage them to use their team's intellectual capital to the company's or organization's advantage.

As I said in the introduction, we business owners keep a scary secret. Sometimes, we are keeping that secret from our team. Employees often imagine the business owner in an upper-floor office with a big window, sitting back with their feet on their desk, thinking they've got it made. They might not realize the enormous stress business owners often carry. If you find yourself in this toxic position, consider joint accountability. Ask others in your organization to hold you accountable, and you can keep them accountable.

Joint accountability provides employees a larger field of view. Years ago, I was doing some offshore fishing, and the boat captain was concerned about a brewing storm. I couldn't see the storm—at that moment, the ocean was as smooth and clear as a sheet of glass. The anglers on the boat began groaning and complaining when the captain ordered a cease fishing call.

But we didn't have the same view as the captain. This boat had radar and an elevated captain's deck, which provided greater visibility, providing the captain comprehensive information. We could only see one perspective, but the captain could see the entire picture, and he knew the bigger mission was getting home safely, over and above catching fish. Even though the fishermen were discouraged about heading back, it quickly became apparent that the captain could see something we couldn't, and he was helping us mitigate risk. Risk reduction is something a company's leadership must do for the company to survive—not only to fish today but to fish another day. Had the people fishing shared the broader view that the captain had, they would have been on the same page from the beginning.

In addition to joint accountability, you might also consider joint responsibilities. If you're trying to build leaders, you can lay out some particularly tough assignments as a test, stretching the person to the extent of their capabilities. Don't forget to give credit where it's due. There's not one person in this world who got to where they are alone.

Businessman and author Arnold Glasow said it well: "A good leader takes a little more than his share of the blame, a little less than his share of the credit."[22] Your team is looking for a leader who isn't just going to share in the good times, they're going to be accountable if the team stumbles. As a business owner, you're going to get credited when your team succeeds— you were the one responsible for the team, after all! Your efforts to uplift others and make them look good will pay off exponentially.

You're Not Raising Your Baby Alone

Let's start with the basics. You were birthed into this world. You had someone who fed you, raised you, and cared for you. You did not get to where you are by yourself.

You might think, "I built this business by myself." But you have customers who helped you get to where you are. You have suppliers, employees, and peers. Never take credit for everything yourself. We business owners did not do this—whatever *this* is—all by our lonesome. Yes, we're the ones taking the risk. I get it. I live it, friend. But whenever you give credit to the team, your team will revel in the accolade, and eventually, they will become leaders.

Up and Down

If there is a clearly defined and understood vision and direction, leadership is being "taught" and "caught." Leadership is working when there is multilevel, multidirectional communication taking place: competency, instead of just directives, flows from the top, and frontline workers are able to influence from the bottom.

If solutions and innovations are flowing from every facet of the organization, your leadership training is working because your members are being leaders. Suppose the janitor, the person who's standing at the assembly line, or the person who's doing data entry brings solutions to frontline problems up chain. In that case, you have multilevel, multidirectional competency. If there's trust all across the organization—frontline, top-line, sideways—then leadership is working.

You're making some strides. You *can* build leaders within your organization. I'll leave you with this question one more time: **in your absence, how effective is your leadership?**

Leaders Motivate and Inspire

On her website, life coach Lisa Haisha says about leadership: "Great leaders don't set out to be leaders. They set out to make a difference. It's never about the role—always about the goal."[23]

Leaders know where they're going. They ask questions. They have a long view. They see the big picture. They're concerned about people.

You may be thinking that I could be describing a manager. But that's not exactly true. There's a classic distinction attributed to Peter Drucker that says "management is doing things right. Leadership is doing the right things."[24] There's a significant difference there. I know it's a play on words but hear me out. People will often think, "I have managers; therefore, I'm driving value." We know we need to get the organization to a place where it doesn't revolve around us, the owners. We know that is the golden goose. We think that hiring managers will improve our company's value, but there are differences between leaders and managers in business.

Managers have policies and procedures. Leaders have visions and strategies.

Usually, managers are not visionaries or strategists. They are trained and paid to follow orders from the top, not to think through processes strategically. But, friends, if you're trying to build leaders within your organization, you want to train employees to think globally and strategically so they can catch the company's vision and help you take it where you want it to go.

Managers take orders and direct people. Leaders motivate and inspire people.

You may say, "Well, I've got managers in my company because they can direct and control situations." True, that's what managers do. They're good army generals. Managers take orders and move and manage people as they see fit to accomplish their directives. However, leaders don't direct or control; they motivate and inspire. Leaders aren't trying to micromanage. Instead of directing and telling people what to do, they cast visions for people to follow willingly. You see, leaders can motivate people to see causes bigger than themselves.

Managers think about what the company has to do. Leaders think about where the company's going.

Managers ask, "What do we have to do?" Leaders ask, "Where are we going?" Managers try to deal with each problem as it comes up, whereas leaders think about problems in a global, long-term context. To increase your company's value, you want to develop leaders who can think contextually and long term. You don't want managers stuck in the immediacy of problems. Instead, you want leaders who can solve short-term problems based on the company's long-term goals.

Managers give directions. Leaders ask questions.

Just as managers receive directions, they give directions and orders to employees under them. They expect employees to listen to what they say and then follow their instructions. Leaders inspire action by asking their team members questions. Rather than saying, "Do this," leaders ask, "Is there a better way to do this? How would you accomplish this?" Or, "May I show you my thoughts on the matter?"

Managers are bottom-line oriented. Leaders are big picture oriented.

Managers focus on the bottom line. They're worried about whether they have made enough profit, products, or revenue for the company. I have fallen into this category too many times myself. Yes, business owners have to focus on the bottom line, but if we can teach our team members to be big picture oriented, we'll add value to our company. Then, instead of asking how much profit or revenue the company has made, your leaders will be asking how the revenue or profits affect the company's future.

Managers worry about projects. Leaders worry about people.

Finally, managers tend to worry about projects, whereas leaders worry about people. Now, caring about your team members doesn't mean you don't demand high output or near perfection. It just means that you care about others more than you do yourself.

Leadership = Value

Leadership is a vital quality for your small business, not just in management but also throughout the company.

Since your leaders understand your company's vision, they can use team members' intellectual property toward that aim. Leaders can place team members in positions that will maximize their effectiveness and efficiency. That puts your company at an advantage over other companies that do not use good leadership skills.

How Leadership Brings Value

The value-maximization process questions below can help you gauge your company's leadership efforts and define areas of focus to help you achieve greater value. The process is covered in more detail in the conclusion.

Your Dream Team

A dream team advisory board provides a system of checks and balances as well as a sense of calm during tough times. A seasoned team can help you identify problems in other business areas, saving you money and time as you address those issues.

The way I look at a dream team of advisors is as a group of individuals you can frequently contact who **are paid** to drive your company's culture and direction. Perhaps it's a financial planner, a CPA, an attorney, and a couple of other business colleagues who sit together on a quarterly or annual basis. Whomever it consists of, they challenge the business owner to subject their plans and ideas to scrutiny by individuals outside of the company.

- Do you have an advisory dream team for your company?
- How often do you meet with your team of advisors?
- Does your team have experience with your type of business and understand the growth phases of your business?
- Does the advisory team actively collaborate with your company's senior management or corporate leadership?
- Does the team have a diversification background in their education and experiences, along with differences in race, religion, sex, and creed?

These questions can help you develop a dream team of advisors committed to your company's value maximization and not just a group of golf buddies who meet up every few months. A good team will help guide strategy and have lots of industry-specific experience, allowing the company to manage risk, navigate industry changes, and maintain compliance. I've seen companies hire experienced businesspeople to their team, but they were prone to making novice mistakes because they had never worked in the particular space.

I have this outside input in my own companies, and let me tell you, it has led to a lot of "aha moments" and invaluable direction in my business. It means I have a lot of bright people available who try to tear my business apart for me so I can get out in front of any issues that might occur. Think of outside leadership like a white-hat hacker trying to break into your systems to find vulnerabilities and make your company stronger. I love being that person, meeting with business owners monthly. We meet every month with our business clients to try to help them move forward.

Regarding your team's makeup, the more diversity, the better because the more angles you can look at something from, the closer you'll be to getting an accurate picture. Think about how police officers gather a group of witnesses to figure out what happened after a car wreck. Officers ask everyone about the same incident, and multiple views provide the most exact picture of what occurred. So, it is best when you have that in your dream team of advisors.

You also want team members who are well seasoned and understand the process. It is reassuring that experienced people are there to help you move through a storm whenever it emerges. In my own company, I lean on people who have gone down this road before. You've probably heard someone say, "Experience is the best teacher." A better piece of wisdom is that someone else's experience is a far better teacher because you can learn from their mistakes without the pain of going through them. If you can get a dream team of advisors who understand your business and the path you need to take to reach your destination, it can help you mitigate and de-risk your company. And decreased risk equals greater value.

As a consultant who works with successful companies across the country, I have the opportunity to view what works and what doesn't. I get to see companies mess up, learn from their failures, and then apply the principle to other companies I'm involved with. If we are not careful, we business owners look "into" the company versus looking "outside" the company. If we look out, then we can see things coming and prepare for them. Applying this one lesson has helped me stay focused on building a highly transferable business.

Organizational Structure

The senior leadership team makes decisions on a day-to-day basis and helps guide the company's strategic-planning efforts. Suppose we can bring along seasoned leaders—with the battle scars to prove their knowledge—who provide calm, resolve, experience, and patience. In that case, the company will flourish far more than with novice leadership. An engaged leadership team can help develop leaders throughout the company, contributing to increased efficiency and profitability—and ultimately, value.

- Does your company have a formal organizational chart?
- Do your employees know who the senior leaders are?
- Do your senior executives (the C-suite including your Chief Executive Officer, Chief Financial Officer and Chief Operations Officer) have experience in running this type of firm, or are they newbies?
- Has the leadership team focused on operational excellence?

Bottom Down, Top Up Communication

Your company's leaders should be able to communicate the company's goals, direction, vision, values, and mission. They should be able to do so at a moment's notice. And they should be aligning the entire organization to that end.

- Does the company have well-documented mission and vision statements?
- Have those statements been clearly and effectively communicated to your employees?
- Have you developed immediate and future objectives? If so, have they been written?
- Is the organization in complete alignment with everyone facing in the same direction?
- Is the company's production and execution of its objectives regularly communicated with employees?
- Have you diagrammed the tactical actions the company must take over the next six or 12 months?
- Do you have performance indicators or performance evaluations applied from the leadership down?
- What kind of example does the leadership team set?

All your team members need to be strong, but your senior leadership team or executive team must be powerful. They are the rock star coaches to the players and the team. If they don't know where you're going, then you'll never get anywhere.

You want to create a respectful, open dialogue so that the janitor and the chair of your dream team can communicate without feeling threatened. I remember sitting in a meeting with a business owner who was a hotshot. This guy had a pedigree. He had graduated from an Ivy League school, he had the looks, the wife, and the car, and he bragged about "his" company and "his" employees. He was using language that isolated him from the organization, and when I began talking with his team, I heard them say, "He doesn't care about what we say. He tells us ideas, and we give feedback, and he doesn't listen. We share our ideas, and he discounts them."

What he showed was that he didn't give a flying flip about what his employees said. This owner could have shared understanding and perspectives with his team, but instead, he looked down on them. The company struggled as a result of his poor communication and distrust.

Organizational Culture

The organization's culture will show if the business is positioned to handle the transition and how much turnover is likely. If you have a high turnover ratio because of poor culture, poor leadership, poor senior management, or a poor board of directors, then you have a problem. It's up to leadership to recognize the factors contributing to the negative culture and take any corrective actions needed.

- Is there a culture of unity and teamwork across multiple disciplines among the employees?
- Does your company actively work to raise up the next generation of leaders?
- Is the company positioned leverage opportunities as they emerge?
- Do employees have their own agendas or are their performances measured against the company's objectives?
- Does the team's culture embrace change?

Planning Your Exit

Spending time trying to position your business to where you can sell it but failing to establish and consistently update an exit plan represents a failure in leadership that could significantly affect your company's value. Many business owners expect to hand their companies to their children, but only about 30 percent of businesses make it to the second generation.[25] I've received many calls from unprepared owners asking for help to increase the company's value in one year or less because the offers they received from prospective buyers were nowhere near the desired price.

Value-maximization planning is good business. Some owners stop focusing on the business if they're looking to exit, putting all their effort behind selling, and when they can't find a buyer, they're left with a struggling business. Had the owner had a plan in place when the offer came about, the company would not have suffered. I also know of dozens of companies where the owner got sick, and no one was there to keep the business going. It's essential to have contingency plans in place, no matter what happens.

- Is there a well-documented exit plan in place, including succession and business continuity plans?
- Has it been brought up to date or modified within the past 12 months?
- Have you pinpointed the future leaders in your organization? If so, how do you plan to refine their skills?
- Have you sought an external perspective to scrutinize your plan? If so, have they provided feedback to help optimize your succession plan?

The Bottom Line

In the coastal area of Georgia, where I grew up, we would see seven- to 10-foot tide variations per day, twice a day. And whenever the tide would go out, it would leave the shore muddy and flat with trickles of water streaming out. But then when the tides came in, in a blue moon or a new moon or red moon, sometimes you would see the marsh grass disappear beneath this ocean of beautiful water due to exceptionally high tide movement.

Everything would rise and fall on the tide. Whenever the shrimp boats were docked at port, they would rise to the tide's highest level. When the tide went back out, they would sink to the mudflats. The tide is leadership in your business, and if you have poor leadership, you're losing value. Whenever we pause to apply good leadership characteristics to our business, we position it for its greatest maximum value.

Action Item: Leadership

Communication is key to successful leadership. Team members need to understand what is expected of them and that everyone is working together. Does everyone understand the overall plan? Getting collective buy-in will make it easier to reinforce priorities. Rethink one-on-one meetings: instead of being a weekly, biweekly, or monthly task, think of one-on-ones as an ongoing conversation to communicate team and personal priorities with individuals.

Be the kind of leader you'd want to work for—instead of thinking of your employees as working for you, think of it as your responsibility to work for them. Their success will become your company's success, and it will drive up the company's value.

CHAPTER 4

Sales: Only the Best for Your Baby

One of the eight major areas of your company is **sales**. To grow your company's value, you must understand what it means to have a best-in-class sales process, team, or division.

Let's Start with a Basic Question: What Is Sales?

All businesses have a sales department, the division of a company that sells products or services.

But what is a sale? Here is the technical definition: *When an obligation is created for a buyer to provide remission in exchange for a product or service.* For a financially simple explanation, I would say a sale is *the process of providing goods or services to another for some form of payment.* (I describe it as "some form of payment" rather than money because sometimes we sell for things other than money. We can also make exchanges, like in a bartering system.)

A Best-in-Class Sales Process Is More Than Order Taking

Years ago, I had the opportunity to consult with a business owner—let's call her Sally—who ran a canine-health consulting company. As I inquired about her company's sales process, she told me about their unbelievable marketing team and great website. "Whenever somebody comes into our marketing funnel, I contact the prospective client. I'm the best salesperson in the company, and I know how to weed out people. I know how to prequalify clients. I know how to decide on which is the best prospective client to take on."

By performing all of these tasks, Sally was positioning herself to where she would have to duplicate herself to increase the company's value. A best-in-class sales process is transferable to other sales individuals, not one that is based on one or two salespeople's personalities. In this particular scenario, I suggested that Sally should break up the sales processes by territory, create a sales pitch that hits different personalities, and create a method to teach rookie salespeople how to communicate this company's values.

But Sally didn't want to let go of the sales process. Even with all of the other order-taking and marketing systems in place, Sally could never move the company away from an *individual* who controls the company's flow to a sales *process*.

A Best-in-Class Sales Process Helps Companies Increase in Value

Remember, we don't necessarily need to increase revenue to increase value. It's more about building and improving a repeatable system. So, what can you or your business leaders do to close more sales than your competitors? Although there are hundreds of things you can do, here are my top-10 ways to create a strong sales structure, based on companies that I see standing apart from the competition in sales.

1. Create clear and concise sales goals. Don't ramble on or make your goals too hard to understand. People often say, "Make your sales goals monumental. Make them so hard that you can't achieve them." I don't know if I agree with that because it might create a mentality of failure if your goals are unattainable. I like the term "B-HAG": big, hairy, audacious goals. Jim Collins came up with that term for his 1994 book *Built to Last*.[26] I think everybody should have one big, hairy, audacious goal. I heard somebody say that he wanted his company to be featured in a Super Bowl ad. That's a big goal. I listened to another person say that he wants his birthday to be a holiday when he dies. That's a big, hairy, audacious goal, but how achievable is it? (Not to mention, it's entirely out of his control and up to others to create the holiday.) If your sales goals aren't possible, you're going to lose motivation among your sales personnel, your marketing division, and your whole company.

2. Make reasonable sales goals that your team can achieve on a regular basis. You shouldn't be able to hit your sales goals every time. If you do, then your goals are too low. However, if you fail to meet your goals regularly, then your goals are too high. It's challenging to suggest the right success rate, but you shouldn't always reach your goals or always miss them.

3. Play up your company's competitive advantage. Every team member should be able to articulate your company's competitive advantage. What makes your company stand out? What makes it different, special, unique? That message needs to be evident throughout your company.

4. Have your sales team provide regular feedback to the marketing department. If planted seeds aren't growing, the farmer needs to know why. I grow a garden in rocky soil in East Tennessee. There's a famous country song, "Rocky Top," that has the lines: "Corn won't grow at all on Rocky Top/Dirt's too rocky by far." I'm finding how tough it truly is to grow corn in the rocky soil, and I have a horticulture degree! I want to go out there, slap some seeds in the ground, and go back to reap the harvest, but that's not how it works. From the time the seed is planted, you need to nurture it: make sure the corn patch doesn't blow over in the wind, keep your green beans strung up properly, and keep the bugs off your plants. That's like a sales process. One day the gardener, in this case, a salesperson, can pick produce off something they've been working on for some time. If the produce isn't growing, then the marketing department needs to know why. So many times, that's missed.

5. Win big deals without reducing your profit margins. Don't cut your price to win big deals. Learn to win them without haggling so you can keep your profit margins high. Do you think Apple, a trillion-dollar company, is going to cut their price because you haggle? No, the price is what the price is, so your sales process has to win big deals. Great companies know their worth and stick to it.

6. Maintain a robust pipeline of prospects. Know who your target market is and where they live. Then, follow up if they don't buy your product or use your service the first time. So many times, as order takers, we will get somebody's name when they contact us, and we'll follow up with them once or twice. That's not a maintenance program for prospects. A robust line of prospects means knowing the target market. I know there are 50,000 school-age children in Knox County, Tennessee. If I'm trying to sell backpacks, I should know every parent, every zip code, and every house where parents live. And I should have a way to get my bags in front of those parents. When the parents inquire about my backpacks for the first time, I should be prepared to strategically follow up to keep our backpacks front and center of their minds.

7. Use your pipeline to forecast your revenue. You should have the ability to review your sales funnel or pipeline and predict how much income your company will receive over X amount of time. Each industry will be different, but you should be able to forecast how much revenue you're going to receive in a predictable format.

8. Keep employee turnover low. With clear, achievable goals and achievement incentives, you can keep more of your salespeople. That prevents you from having to train new hires continually. It also gives your sales team members time to perfect their skills.

9. Keep customer retention high. Just as you want to keep employees, you need to keep customers. Having repetitive customers makes your revenue more predictable and your sales goals more achievable.

10. Work as a team instead of individuals. Finally, prevent cutthroat sales practices by encouraging teamwork among your sales team.

Now that you have reviewed the above 10 attributes, how does your company stack up? Do you have a best-in-class sales structure, or are you an order taker?

Through the Funnel

To refuel my tractor, I go to the store and fill up several five-gallon cans to take back to the farm. Let me tell you, those cans are heavy. My Kubota tractor's fuel tank is located on the hood section, a good four and a half or five feet up there. I have to climb up on the tire, lugging this big ol' thing of diesel. If you've ever tried to pour a lot of fuel into a little hole by yourself, you know it's nearly impossible. So, I use a funnel. A funnel helps to take the splashing and sloshing out of the equation. The funnel I use is probably about 14 inches across, and it fits perfectly down into the fuel-tank opening. My dad taught me an old trick to keep trash from going into the fuel: take an old pair of pantyhose and stretch it across the opening. That way, as I'm pouring the fuel into the funnel, any contaminants that might be in the five-gallon container won't go into the tractor's fuel tank.

As I pour, I don't have to focus on where the fuel is hitting the funnel because it moves a large, irregular flow into a small little opening with consistency. It's what a funnel is designed to do. Funnels work the same way with sales. If you **look at your sales process as a funnel**, many prospective clients will enter the funnel's wide end, but you need to get *qualified clients* to exit through the narrow end. In other words, many potential customers will hear about your goods and services, but few will buy. The key to a sales process is getting your potential customers through your funnel in a smooth, consistent, and steady flow.

The Steps in a Traditional Sales Process

Traditionally, salespeople follow a process when customers walk through a business door. They

- meet the customer,
- qualify the customer's needs,

- show the customer their product or explain their service,
- discuss cost,
- do a trial close,
- listen to customer objections,
- handle customer objections, and
- listen to follow-up objections.

These steps lead to the salesperson either closing the sale or allowing the customer to walk away. The salesperson's goal is to bring the customer to an immediate yes or no answer.

Think About the Traditional Sales Process in Terms of Buying a Car

I walk into the auto dealership and am greeted by a salesperson. The salesperson then listens to my desires. I'm looking for a silver vehicle that has four-wheel drive (because a country boy only buys four-wheel drive) and leather (high class), and I have a specific price point. I have likely been car shopping before I even reach the dealership by reviewing sales ads on the internet.

As a customer, I'm trying to figure out if this salesperson really knows what they're talking about. Do they have my best interest in mind? Are they listening to me? And, in turn, the salesperson is trying to qualify the sale. Can I afford what I'm asking for? The next thing a salesperson will do is talk to me about my needs. They're trying to qualify what I'm looking for.

"I have three kids," I say, so they realize we're probably not dealing with a two-door sedan.

"Do you need an SUV?" they ask.

"My wife drives an SUV, so we don't need another. But I often tow off-road and carry heavy items."

They're trying to narrow me down to qualify my needs.

"Well, Justin, based on what you're saying, we have the Ford F-150, we have the Tundra, and we have the Silverado. We have three different vehicles here that are four-wheel drives and have enough room for your needs."

They go about showing me the vehicles on the lot, and I'm drawn to the towing capacity of the F-150, but I love the interior of the Tundra. I find myself sitting at this salesperson's desk, and they start going through pricing. At this point, there's going to be a trial close. They'll say something like "What can we do to get you in this truck today, Justin?" and I'm going to run through my objections.

Maybe I want to sleep on the decision since I like to think things through. The salesperson will say, "No problem," provide any further information to help me decide, and make a plan to follow up the next day. Maybe I have a subsequent objection, and the salesperson will work to answer it.

If they are a pushy salesperson, my objections don't matter to them—the only thing that matters is seeing me drive off in this vehicle today. The stage is set for me to say yes or no.

The Consumer's Buying Process

Although traditional sales processes do still happen, consumers having access to social media and the internet has transformed the buying process. Most buyers have done their due diligence long before they enter a store. They know the pros and cons of your product. They know what they want to pay and what they think is fair to pay for your service. In fact, according to the global best-practice insights and technology company CEB and Google, 57 percent of the buying process is complete before customers ever contact the supplier or a salesperson gets involved.[27] Once customers walk into a store, salespeople only start with a 43 percent chance of moving customers from their initial contact to the ultimate purchasing decision. That 43 percent is what we're dealing with in the new sales funnel.

Steps in a Modern Sales Process

The traditional sales process operates on the belief that the salesperson or business has 100 percent of the opportunity to sell a product or service. But a modern business in this internet-based world must begin and end sales differently. Assume your potential customers are already knowledgeable and need help choosing among the best options.

You must

- market to your ideal customers,
- relate to your customers,
- determine the customers' needs,
- close the sale, and
- follow up with your customers.

A Different Process

From the get-go, the best-in-class sales process *feels* different. Instead of opting for the traditional sales cycle, the salesperson works to develop a relationship. I recently went into a local CarMax location, and a salesperson walked up to me and said, "My kids are about the same age." That was the first thing he said to me.

He made a connection. He started talking to the kids, asking their names, and giving them candy. He was engaging in a relationship rather than immediately trying to gather what my need was. He had a relationship-style agenda and approached me differently than typical salespeople do when you walk into a store. A generic question like "How can I help you?" is a sign of an order taker.

Only after he established the relationship did he begin finding compelling reasons for me to work with him. He asked me if I had looked anywhere else and if I wanted to buy a new or used vehicle.

"There's nothing wrong with buying a new car. But you know what? Cars depreciate about 18 percent when they come off the lot."

"Actually," I said, "it's more like 20 to 30 percent by the end of the first year."

"Oh, okay, so you've done your homework. So you know why it's always best to buy used."

He was also trying to find compelling reasons for me to make my decision and gain a commitment.

"Justin, when do you think you need to make this decision?"

"You know, that's a great question. I certainly appreciate you asking," I said. He wasn't trying to push me; he was trying to understand my timeline. "I don't do anything very quickly. I'm more analytical. I like to think things through," I said.

"Okay, Justin, if I find a vehicle that fits your parameters, can I text that to you?"

"Please," I said. "Feel free."

He texted me three times over the course of three weeks without being overbearing. When I come to a point where I will decide to move forward and close the sale, I'm more likely to work with the CarMax salesperson because of his approach.

Regardless of whether a prospective customer or client moves forward with you to make the deal, follow-up is crucial to a best-in-class sales process. When someone buys a product or service from you, you want it to be a good experience. You want to have positive testimonials. If someone says, "You know what, now's not the time," or, "No, I'm not going to buy from you," you have to follow up. You want to know *why* they didn't buy from you. Did they buy from a competitor instead? If so, why?

Most people are order takers, but your goal is to greet customers at every step of their discovery process, all the way through until they purchase from you. When they make the purchase, you'll be there to thank them and have a postsale follow-up to continue to nurture the relationship. I know people who have bought cars from the same person for decades. Trust is difficult to manufacture. Being able to move customers through the sales funnel efficiently can transform your company.

Herding the Cats

Many times, managing salespeople can feel like herding cats. Remember the DiSC assessment model? Salespeople are often strong *I* personalities but can also have *D* traits. They love working with people and want to conquer the world in which they work. They're decisive, focused, and purpose-driven individuals. So how in the world do you manage a group of people with I and *D* personalities? Generally, managers use the following approach: set short-term goals, plan how salespeople will meet those goals, track sales performance, and evaluate sales performance.

I recommend tweaking the typical approach a bit. If you are managing a best-in-class sales team, you need to use a best-in-class management process. Therefore, I recommend that my clients use the TEAM methodology to manage their sales teams, a tactic I learned in my CVGA training. Allow me to explain.

T—Tasks

When you create a successful sales team, you need to give the members specific **tasks**. Hold them accountable for accomplishing the tasks daily, weekly, monthly, quarterly, and yearly. Ask team members to search for potential customers, qualify them, set appointments, stick to agendas, give presentations, and ask for referrals. By providing team members quantifiable **tasks**, you can measure their achievements and monitor their growth.

E—Expertise

Next, expect greatness from your team members—demand **expertise**. For your team to sell a product or service, they must know everything possible about what they're selling. They must know how to answer questions, solve problems, and get around objections. If they don't know what they're selling, they're not going to make sales. They can't take costumers through the sales funnel and end with a successful close unless they're **experts** in their field.

A—Attitude

Another way to create a best-in-class sales team is to expect a positive **attitude**. People can't choose their circumstances, but they can choose the attitude they have about their circumstances. As a business owner, you want your team members' behaviors and attitudes to reflect your organization's culture and ethos. One bad apple *can* spoil the rest of the bunch and reflect poorly on your organization. Demand a positive **attitude** from your team members. And if you have a bad apple, don't be afraid to remove it.

One of my heroes in life was my youth pastor, Kirk Branch. Out of the many lessons he taught, one has forever influenced me. He said, "Your attitude is your choice." Man, that simple statement has rung in my mind thousands of times since I first heard it. Some people say, "The attitude of gratitude" or just, "Be grateful in all things." The author, salesman, and speaker Zig Ziglar said, "Your attitude, not your aptitude, will determine your altitude."[28] A sales team must have a positive attitude.

M—Management

Finally, make sure you teach your sales team members how to **manage** themselves. Have them hold themselves accountable and responsible for their actions, tasks, and systems. Make them track the results of those activities and have them deliver the reports to you. The more they **manage** themselves, the less you as a business owner have to micromanage them.

In your organization, are you trying to create a best-in-class team? Are you managing your sales team using TEAM (tasks, expertise, attitude, and management) or another system? If you're not, then you will never have the sales team you need to build long-term value in your business.

Help in Raising Your Baby

Your baby deserves the best. Think of your salespeople as teachers and tutors helping your baby reach its potential. Maybe you tour a few schools or interview several tutors, babysitters, or daycare providers to find the perfect match. When you're interviewing, you will see how your baby—your business—responds to each of them.

Think of these people as an extension of yourself, a chance to reinforce your goals in your absence. Sometimes a hire turns out to be a bad match, and it's essential to be vigilant in taking corrective action or replacing them. But if you've done your homework throughout the hiring process and hired the best people, you shouldn't need to worry too much. Although you can keep a close watch over everything, you also want to allow the people you've hired to do what they do best. And what they should do best is help you raise your baby.

The Perfect Match

Having a great sales team is easy if you hire great salespeople. You must pick people who understand that consumers don't want to deal with overly pushy salespeople. They don't want products or services shoved down their throats. Today's consumers desire solutions that your company provides for their problems —and only when they need them. It is the job of best-in-class salespeople to understand this in their sales process.[29] That means it is even more critical that you know how to pick the best-in-class performers for your sales team. If you have salespeople who are only out for themselves, then a negative culture can creep into your organization. Whenever you're building a best-in-class sales team, the salespeople have to fit in with the company's culture. No ifs, ands, or buts.

So how in the world do you hire the "right" salespeople? How do you weed out the sour apples from your batch of potential hires?

Understand the type of person you're looking to hire.

Right off the bat, you have to know what you expect from your salespeople. What kind of work ethic do you want them to have? Are you going to demand excellence from them? How do you expect them to interact with potential customers, clients, and other team members? To whom will they be accountable? You must know the type of person you're looking for before you hire new team members.

Start the screening process.

Once you know who you're looking for, it's time to start the employee screening process. As people apply for your open position, have them take a **personality assessment like the DiSC assessment or 16 Personalities**, and follow it up with a values assessment like **Barrett's Personal Values Assessment**. Then, review the assessments' results to see if any of the applicants' personalities and values fit in with the culture of your company.

Have an initial face-to-face interview.

Conduct a face-to-face interview with applicants who passed your screening process. Review the results of the assessments with them. What do they say about themselves as a candidate? What do they leave out? Detail the expectations that you created in Step 1 to see how they respond.

Do they have positive attitudes and team-oriented mentalities? Are they up front and responsive to the behavioral assessment? Use this time to vet out candidates whose attitudes and values don't align with your core values or your company's ethos.

Meet again for sales role-playing.

Typically, if applicants "pass" Step 3, you will ask them to return for a second face-to-face meeting. This time, you want to test their sales skills. You want them to "sell" you a product or service so you can assess how they interact with customers. Are they too pushy or too passive? Can they handle the pressure? Additionally, you want to see if they're experts in this field. Do they know your products or services? Can they sell you something as simple as a pen?

Inspect prior sales activities.

Before you offer sales applicants employment in your company, you want to inspect their prior sales activities. Ask for commission and income verification. Call their references. Look at their calendars and schedules. In other words, make sure your potential sales hires aren't "selling" you false information.

You must take your time and hire the right salespeople—this is your baby we're talking about here! Be slow about finding best-in-class salespeople because you can only build a best-in-class sales team if you hire right. If you hire wrong, you better be quick to fire. You don't have any time to lose when you're trying to increase your business's value. Remember: only the best for your baby.

You Get What You Pay For

If you've been in business for any length of time, you probably get a little flustered trying to create competitive and fair compensation plans for your employees, especially your salespeople. Pay can be extremely rewarding when it is competitive and very frustrating when it is not. Employees pay close attention to their compensation plans. If you make changes to their plans, *your* plans may backfire. To protect yourself, you must know what needs to be in a best-in-class sales compensation plan.

Before you put compensation plans together for your team members, you must understand their importance. Good compensation plans can

- increase team morale,
- magnify and encourage an outstanding work ethic,
- reinforce team participation,
- enhance multidirectional communication through your organization,
- promote the exchange of useful information,
- improve the overall sales of the company, and
- increase the business's gross profit.

What do you need to know to meet the compensation objectives?

Step 1: Know how much your competition pays their top salespeople.

- Do they pay commission or salary?
- Is commission based on a percentage of gross sales or gross profit?
- Do similar companies pay expenses for their salespeople?
- How do others calculate total compensation?

Step 2: Decide what compensation and benefits you will offer.

- Take time to consider the long-term ramifications and rewards of your compensation package.
- Have the compensation plan reflect your core values.
- Use compensation to instill loyalty in team members.
- Decide whether you will offer salespeople commission, salary, or salary plus commission.
- Create realistic long-term and short-term benefit/incentive plans.

Evaluating Your Sales Compensation Plan Model

As you're considering compensation and benefits options, keep the following things in mind for your plan:

- Calculate commission based on gross profit rather than gross sales.

- Increase compensation as sales increase.
- Reward the hard workers and producers.
- Allow salespeople to criticize the compensation plan constructively.
- Make sure the plan provides a living income for salespeople.
- Keep the sales manager selling until you reach seven full-time salespeople.
- Reevaluate your plan often as your business grows and the market changes.

To attract and keep top salespeople, you must offer them a best-in-class compensation plan. It must meet marketplace standards and align with your business's core values. If your plan promotes both friendly competition and loyalty, you can improve your company's overall sales, which should increase your salespeople's compensation. Be fair and be generous. Your team members help you achieve success.

How Sales Bring Value

The sample value-maximization process questions below can help you gauge your company's sales efforts and define areas of focus to help you achieve greater value. The process is covered in more detail in the conclusion.

Sales Team Compacity

- Where is your sales footprint?
- Is the reach of your company's sales team regional, domestic, or global?

It's important to define your sales reach and target region, otherwise, your sales efforts could become muddled, or you could spend effort focusing on areas that undermine your company's reach or penetration.

The broader your customer base, the less risky your company is. Think about a landscaping company: if it had all of its business on one street and a tornado struck that street, it could lose 100 percent of its business in one horrific event. Whereas if the company had customers spread out within the neighborhood, or across town, or in different cities, the risk is much lower.

Not too long ago in Knoxville, Tennessee, we had a hailstorm that came through and damaged many cars and houses with golf ball–sized hail. Local insurance companies then had issues because they had too many clients concentrated in affected areas.

Sales Leaders

- Have you identified the salespeople in your business? Who regularly secures jobs or sales?
- How experienced is your sales team?
- Does your company have a training process for new hires and an internal sales methodology?

A huge red flag in business occurs when the business owner is the company's best salesperson. It's dangerous when you're the top salesperson for your company because then those contacts, lead sources, or centers of influence, as we often call them, are going to be focused on the business owner alone. It would be best to build a sales team, have an executive manage them, and break the group up across your target area, be it in a state, region, or country. Then, in time, you'll have various people with years of experience selling. You'll have veterans there.

Additionally, create diversity among your sales team. For example, the last thing you need is for your entire sales department to retire simultaneously, requiring a complete replacement of the entire sales team in a short amount of time. If you have a sales team that can sell the company's product or services, has low turnover rates, and has an internal sales methodology and training process, you've built something that can be scaled up or down. You've created something that can be duplicated.

Sales System

- Is there a written plan for your company's sales? Does it include metrics to measure your sales team's success?
- Do your marketing strategies complement the separate sales plan?
- How well do your strategies reflect your business plan, mission, and values?

Which team members are going to execute the sales system?

Whenever you deal with sales, you're trying to figure out how you can take your product and enter into other markets. Only after you know the exact target can you then move forward. It is not a case of ready ... fire ... aim.

Sales system is all about the process of taking the company from where you are today to where you want to be. Many companies sell to anybody who can fog a mirror and, in doing so, they end up with very inefficient customers. If you become laser-focused on who your most profitable customer is and build a sales strategy around them, you become highly efficient.

Sales Processes

- What projections are your sales team expected to produce? Do you have targets and forecasts?
- Are you equipped to achieve and solidify key performance indicators (KPIs)?
- How many sales are taking place every quarter or semiannually?
- Is there a relationship built between your sales and marketing teams? Does the relationship extend to their initiatives?
- What percentage of leads result in sales?
- How is automation used in the sales process?
- Have you identified the exact steps your organization uses from when a potential customer enters the funnel to the end of the relationship?
- Have you integrated the sales process with the marketing process to create hyper-efficiency?

Sales processes is just functionality—it's how your company's sales system works. Operational efficiency comes after detailed process development.

Sales processes specifically influence the people who are carrying out the strategy. If you build the sales operations correctly, the members of your sales team will know exactly how they're going to be judged and motivated. Salespeople love competition.

Sales Reporting

- Have you identified your sales trends across the last five years?
- What are your projections for the next five years?
- Do you see an increase or decrease in your projections for the next 12 months? Why?
- How does the sales mix of your products and services influence your projections?
- Are there any economic factors that might cause your sales process to be hampered or hindered?

It all comes down to forecasting so that you, the business owner, and eventually your company's buyer can observe your company's sales avenues. Here's where it gets fun. If you perform forecasting year after year after year, you're able to track what you've projected in the past against the actual results. When you sit down with a buyer, you can show them your pitch book, and they'll have confidence that your pitch book is accurate, which will yield you a higher price. By demonstrating that the business systematically meets your projections, you, in turn, convey assurance and safety to a buyer. This action is similar to the guidance a publicly traded company releases to its shareholders.

Customer Segmentation

- Are you concentrating on reaching clients in any particular region or market?
- What percentage of sales would be lost if your top 10 clients walked away? Could the company survive?
- How would your business respond if you lost the bottom 20 clients?
- What are the obstacles preventing your company from expanding its client base?

Through your sales system, you can identify whether you lost or gained clients and the quality of the client demographics. Having a strong, segmented client base means having client diversity. You don't want to have a concentration issue. A client of ours had one big client who was producing about 35 percent of his company's revenue. He sincerely thought about canceling all his other customers because this one was so much better. Thank goodness he didn't cancel all of his other customers and service, because the large customer ended up leaving him. The client took a hit, but we had already recognized the concentration issue to position him to make more significant profits long term and keep the company afloat even without his large customer.

The Bottom Line

Your sales process adds value because it removes the business owner from the center of the sales process. It will take what's in the business owner's head and put it into a process. It forces them to entrust their baby with somebody else.

If the sales process is tracking a client from the time they come onto your radar to the time they say yes to the time they move into a retention base or provide you a referral, you will know the detailed life cycle of a client. When you see the life cycle, you can hone, strengthen, and tighten it.

To add value, you need to illustrate your sales process on a granular level, step-by-step, with your sales regions and sales team identified and sales regions divided. We consult for a landscaping company that's rocking this process, to the extent that we've divided up the owner's sales regions into subregions that each have specialized sales teams and have incentivized them based on the area. If you go through your team, regions, strategy, operations, projections, and client base and bring it all together, you will have created a sales process that can be duplicated, scaled, and transferred.

Action Item: Sales

What is special about your company? What do you do that no other company can? Understanding the value that your company provides to your clients and communicating that value will set your company apart and drive sales growth.

CHAPTER 5

Marketing: Beautifying Your Baby

Marketing is the process of getting customers interested in your company's products or services. If this sounds essential ... well, it is!

Every year in November, I get excited waiting for the Bass Pro Shops Black Friday sales catalog to hit my mailbox. I love that store—maybe not quite as much as pizza, but it's pretty close. The catalog highlights all the goodies that will be on sale, but I usually look on the Bass Pro Shops website before the email has even arrived. When the time comes that I get my list of deals in the mail, I visit the store and wind up spending more than I ever intended. It happens every year, and I look forward to it!

Because I visit the Bass Pro Shops website regularly, I'm bound to find a third-party advertisement highlighting their specials for cool boots and hats and hunting supplies whenever I go online. My interests align pretty closely with what Bass Pro Shops sells. Still, their robust, targeted advertising ensures that I will buy my supplies with them instead of some other company or online retailer. That's marketing.

The website Lexico, which is powered by Oxford University Press, describes marketing as "the action or business of promoting and selling products or services including market research and advertising."[30] That means that marketing is present during all business stages, from the beginning to the end. Marketing shares similarities with sales, which we've covered. But marketing is different in some important ways.

In the 1960s, marketing professor and author E. Jerome McCarthy developed a basic framework for marketing called the "4 *P*s of marketing."[31] In 1981, Booms and Bitner added three more *P*s to the marketing mix.[32] However, I believe there are more than seven elements to modern marketing. I suggest there are nine *P*s.

Marketing is about how prospective customers connect with you, and it matters to your business. Without marketing, your business cannot gauge potential customer interest and design capacity for growth. Missing marketing will diminish the value of your asset, your business, drastically dropping your sales price.

The Nine Ps: The Elements of Modern Marketing

1. Product

To market your *product* or service, you first have to ask yourself several questions.

- Do you know your product well enough to sell it to customers?
- Who needs your product or service?
- Does this product fit into your marketplace?
- What messaging will help you increase sales of the product?
- Can you develop or modify the product to make it better or more appealing?
- How will you sell your product?
- What platforms will you use?

Essentially, you want to make your product marketable, and to do that, you need to know your product inside and out, how it's useful, and your ideal customer. And no, your ideal customer isn't "all Americans" or "everyone."

2. Price

The second *P* of marketing is *price*. Your marketing team will check out your competitor's pricing and use focus groups or surveys to estimate the price customers are willing to pay for your product. If the price is too high, you will lose your customer base. If it's too low, your company won't capitalize on sales and will end up leaving money on the table. Neither of those options makes your business profitable, much less valuable, so you must consider price when you're marketing.

3. Place

Location, location, location—the *place* can have a massive effect on marketing. How and where will you market your product? Will you sell it strictly through an e-commerce site, or will you have a brick-and-mortar store as well? Will you sell your products on television through QVC or on social media? Before you can advertise your products, you must have a place people can go to purchase them.

4. Promotion

The last *P* identified by McCarthy in the 1960s is *promotion*. Once you know where customers can buy your products or services, you need to promote them through advertising. Maybe you use social media, direct mailers, television, or radio. Perhaps you go to networking events or host them yourself. The goal of promotion is to generate more sales leads by showing off your product or service.

5. People

Added to the list in 1981 is *people*. People run your business from the front lines, the phone lines, or via the internet. Everyone from your maintenance staff to your managing directors meet and greet customers. Their attitudes may not affect whether customers come into your store, but they will affect whether the customers come back. Your team members reflect your company's culture and can therefore be your greatest marketing asset or downfall.

6. Process

The marketing *process* deals with capturing people and ushering them into the sales process. Going back to the study we reviewed in our sales chapter, potential customers have already gone through 57 percent of the buying process before contacting the supplier or involving a salesperson.[33] If the sales process is like a ladder, the marketing process has to get leads to that first rung.

7. Physical Evidence

It's relatively easy to market *physical* products, but it's a bit harder to market intangible services. Technically, you don't have anything to show customers. They can't pick up your services and try them on for size. To market your intangible services, you need to create something tangible that describes, explains, or represents your service process. Maybe you create a chart that shows your service process or a graph that illustrates your service offerings. Give them something physical they can touch and evaluate. During my landscaping days, I spent hours developing a landscaping plan for each client; it was nothing more than words and shapes on a piece of vellum paper, which is translucent like wax paper. I'd use my drafting pencils on the vellum to create overlays. That experience helped me recognize that selling the invisible was about relating to a buyer's dream and helping them visualize their goal's success.

8. Productivity

Perhaps the most controversial *P* of marketing, but one I think belongs on the list, is *productivity*. Measuring the productivity of your marketing campaigns is vital to the success of your marketing department. Your marketing department is trying to read the marketplace and offer goods and services in a way that will appeal to it. Your company's increase or decrease in sales should show the strength of the marketing campaign. Tracking, quantifying, and supporting your marketing results will help you uncover what works and why, and where your company's value lies. You'll be able to show a future buyer the actions you took and the outcomes that resulted. They will then be able to use that information as market research as they try to recast the company's direction.

9. Profitability

I'd argue that *profitability* should be at the top of the list of *P*s. Unless the marketing plan and process leads to profitability, then you're wasting your money. You need your marketing campaigns to be productive *and* profitable, not just productive. Tracking the profitability of your marketing plan helps you assess how your dollars have been spent. I rarely see business owners tracking the return on investment (ROI) of their marketing, so they often have trouble putting the results into context and end up with a "feeling" that marketing doesn't work.

These nine *P*s have all the core elements you need to develop a marketing plan to get your products or services in front of your potential buyers.

Does Marketing Work?

One of the most underused methods of growing your business's value is marketing, but you can't just run out and start slinging money at random marketing options. You need a plan.

I'll give you an example. I have a dental clinic client whose numbers on their income statement (or P&L) just didn't look right. When we started talking about advertising, I asked what kind of results they were seeing. The phone got quiet—as quiet as a summer night when you only hear crickets or frogs out in the distance. Eventually, they said, "Justin, marketing doesn't work."

"Okay … is it that marketing doesn't work, or could it be that you haven't used marketing properly?" I asked. I then asked to look at the company's marketing plan. More crickets.

"Well, we don't have one," they said, after a pause. Welp, there was the problem.

So, we spent some time developing a marketing plan. Fast-forward two years, and they're having the best year in their company's history, and a big part is because of their marketing plan.

A marketing plan is critical for long-term success. It helps you adjust to market saturation, disruption, drift, and flow. When changes happen in marketing—if one segment of your marketing dries up, for example—you need to quickly adjust to avoid wasting marketing efforts or budget on something that isn't working.

As business owners, we often plan mentally or subconsciously, but marketing is one area where you have to slow down and put everything in writing. Every step in the planning process should be deliberate if you want to grow your company's value.

There Are Three Basic Steps to Creating a Marketing Plan:

- **Make a goal**. What is it you want to accomplish? Do you want to increase your profitability by $100 per customer? Do you want to increase your customer base from 1,000 to 1,500?
- You need to **identify the challenges you will face** as you try to achieve your goal. Are your current customers uninterested in high-end procedures or products? Have you tapped out on available customers in your zip code?
- You must **know who your target audience is**. "Anyone who breathes" doesn't help. Get specific. Know your target consumer's age, gender, likes, dislikes, pain points, and more. The better you know your audience, the better you can market to them.

To illustrate this point, and as I mentioned earlier, the persona target audience for my company is called Frazzled Frank, the business owner who's saying, "I have a successful business, but I've never run an X-sized business before. How do I grow it? How do I build a net worth in this business? And how do I position my business so that in the future I can sell it for a profit and make this illiquid asset liquid?"

You don't want to work until you're dead. You want to enjoy life at some point. **You want to run the business, not have the business run you.** These are some of the most common areas of concern for business owners like Frank. They're not new on the scene; they've seen just about every sales

CREATING A MARKETING PLAN

First, you make a goal.

Is it you want to accomplish? Do you want to increase your profitability by $100 per customer? Do you want to increase your customer base from 1,000 to 1,500?

Second, you need to identify the challenges you will face as you try to achieve your goal.

Are your current customers uninterested in high-end procedures or products? Have you tapped out on available customer in your zip cope?

Last, you must know who your target audience is.

"Anyone who breathes" doesn't help. Get specific. Know your target consumer's age, gender, likes, dislikes, pain points, and more. The better you know your audience, the better you can market to them.

pitch in the marketplace. They know what it's like to receive input that is a waste of time and energy. They also see the value in listening to wisdom, receiving counsel, and learning from people who've been down the road before.

Many of these Frazzled Franks are between the ages of 40 and 60. They may have a 10- to 15-year window before they want to get out. Maybe it's less than that. They love to hunt and fish as their hobbies. They like to get outdoors camping. Some are highly educated, and others barely got out of high school. They value knowledge, and they value knowledge applied. They see the value in a coach, a mentor, or a guide. They have clear goals on what they want to accomplish. They're driven.

But they're frazzled!

Digging Deeper

Once you've identified your target market, you have to figure out how to get your product or service in front of them. Here is how you do that:

- **Research your competition**. Who are your competitors? Are they geographically close to you? How do they compare on the internet? Why are they your competition? What do they offer that you don't? How are they marketing differently from you?

- **Create a targeted message**. What does your target market need? Does your product or service make their lives better? How? What value does your product or service bring them?

- **Examine your tactics and advertising channels**. How will you get your message in front of your target market? Will you use social media? Print advertising? Television, radio, YouTube, blogs, public speaking, word of mouth? What would your target market be most likely to see or hear?

- **Set a budget**. How much money are you willing to spend? Will you spend a percentage of your gross revenue or profits?

- **Use metrics to grade your results**. How will you judge the results of your marketing campaign? Will you analyze increased revenue?

Will you measure your results by the number of followers on your social media accounts or by something else?

Stand Apart

Ultimately, you must do more than other businesses to make your marketing plan advantageous to your company. To set your marketing plan and your business apart from others, I recommend doing the following things:

- **Implement and integrate your sales strategy into your marketing plan.** Listen to your sales team and work with them to understand how well the marketing efforts are working for them when they're communicating with customers.
- **Document your marketing plan and its results.** Keep track of what you try and how well it works.
- **Tie your marketing plan into your business goals.** Use marketing to accomplish one or more of your business goals.
- **Reference your marketing plan often.** Don't build one and throw it on the shelf. Have it visible to all team members at all times so they are familiar with the plan.
- **Make your marketing plan a living document.** As you establish what works and what doesn't work, revise your plan accordingly.

Any business owner can do marketing, but it takes a savvy company to track, revise, and follow through with a real plan. The companies that utilize a marketing plan effectively can increase sales and increase their value. So, what are you doing to utilize your marketing plan?

The Value of Positioning

The number 1,018 probably doesn't mean a lot to you unless your birthday happens to fall on October 18, or you were born at 10:18 a.m.

That number happens to be my chess ranking.

When I was about 10 years old, my mom signed my brother and me up for chess classes. A homeschooling father was teaching chess to his sons, and it grew into a chess club. So yes, yours truly was a member of a chess club, and we learned the basics. We learned that the queen is the most powerful on the board (which is not that different from life, is it?). We learned that you can sacrifice pawns. We learned various gambits, gambits declined, and alternative moves designed to surprise your opponent. We had a blast. We all showed up carrying our rolled-up boards, our pieces, and our time clocks and had tournaments almost every week.

As I learned the basics of chess, I participated in a couple of tournaments sponsored by the United States Chess Federation. At one of the sponsored contests when I was 11 or 12 years old, I ended up beating a 16-year-old who was the master of that particular tournament. I beat him, and it was awesome.

At chess tournaments, you typically start with a score of zero, and your score increases as you beat opponents, especially those with a higher ranking than you. Grandmasters or senior masters have a score of 2,400. The lowest rank you can have is what they call a Class J, and that's a score of 100. My score of 1,018 put me in Class E, which is respectable but not too high. I was proud of it anyway.

Chess taught me a valuable concept: **positioning**. Sometimes players take multiple turns to try to set up a capture. Lots of times, you're thinking ahead five, six, seven, sometimes 10 moves as you're trying to position your pieces on the board, all with the ultimate goal of putting your opponent's king in a position where they can no longer move. As your opponent moves their pieces around the table, you're counteracting those moves and trying to gain the best position as an attacker.

Just like pieces on the chessboard, a key area for marketing your company involves positioning. When your customers or prospective customers think about you and your company, what is their impression? What would you like them to think about? How do they perceive you compared to the competition? **Is there a keyword or phrase by which you want your company to be known?** Essentially, your marketing techniques determine your positioning within your industry. You must take active strides to keep it strong or to make it stronger.

Surveying the Market

You're playing a figurative chess game with your competitors. One of you will checkmate the other in the marketing battle. Within the game of business, are you on the offensive or the defensive? Do you know the caliber of your opponent? Have you surveyed their strengths and weaknesses? Have you surveyed your own? To determine your marketing position in comparison to other companies, you must take two types of surveys: the internal market survey and the external market survey.

Internal Market Survey

First, you want to look internally. Start with your company's leaders, whether you're a solo entrepreneur or have an entire management team.

- Do they fit the keyword or phrase that you want your company to be associated with?
- Do they exemplify integrity, innovation, compassion, diligence, efficiency, or whatever keyword describes your company?
- What about your employees?
- Are they people of integrity, innovation, compassion, diligence, or efficiency?
- Your team members are at the front line of your marketing efforts, so are they modeling the behaviors and traits that you want to associate with your company?
- Do their traits or behaviors reveal your company's keyword?

External Market Survey

After you perform a self-assessment of your company and its employees, it's time to get feedback from your customers. Survey customers and let them tell you what they value about your business.

- What reasons do they give for being drawn to your company over a competitor?
- Do they see your company as compassionate or cutting edge?

- What do your customers think about your company?
- Is there a word that describes your company that stands out to them?

Send out actual surveys to your customers to find out what they think of when they think of your company. Read the testimonials left on Google and social media. Positive reviews can suggest the strengths you can build on; negative reviews can offer you ways your company needs improvement.

You are surveying others to determine what they think about your company. What makes you stand out from your competition? Do customers feel about you the way you want them to? Do you have a solid footing within your marketplace, or are customers still trying to figure out what you do best?

Pressure Your Opponent and Improve Your Position

If you're unsure where you stand within your marketplace, you can take steps to find out. Going back to chess for a moment, you need to figure out how you can move faster than your opponent. Hit the time clock and push the pressure back on them, and hopefully, they'll become stressed as you make your position stronger. You can claim a position by doing the following things:

- **Have a positioning statement.** Write out and share your **mission statement**, proclaiming what you're trying to accomplish as a company.
- **Understand your competition's offerings**. Know what marketing moves they're making so you can make your movements offensive rather than defensive.
- **Actively communicate with your customers**. Position your company and offerings for your prospective customers in multiple ways, multiple times a year.
- **Survey your customers.** Ask customers for feedback. What do they want to see from you? How many times would they like to

hear from you?

- **Find ways to enhance your customer experience.** Always be on the lookout for ways to make your customers' experience better.

Let me ask you this: Have you defined the experience you want your customers to have? Start by writing it out in story form. Remember, market positioning is a proactive process; it's not a defensive mechanism or position. To set yourself apart in the marketplace, you must purposefully design your image. You are responsible for how others see you, and that image is formed primarily through marketing. In chess and marketing, good positioning will help you make better moves and give you the best possible opportunity to succeed.

Branding Is Everywhere

Branding is a crucial aspect of marketing. It lets customers instantly recognize what your company stands for.

Branding is everywhere. I consider myself a weekend farmer—someone who does farm work during my free time, separate from my professional duties. One of the animals that I have yet to purchase is a cow. We have goats, chickens, turkeys—all sorts of fun animals. We have three kids who act like cows sometimes, but we don't have an actual cow.

Recently, in Idaho, we spent time with some guides, and I noticed a brand from a branding iron that had been scorched into the wood in the bunkhouse of one of the guides. I learned about branding and how cows range in that part of the country, sometimes with two or three herds together. The cows are branded so that they can tell whose cows belong to who.

We see branding in business too, and frequently we see it without even knowing what it is. Yet, if I describe certain brands, I'm positive you can guess the companies behind them. For instance, if you see a giant red *N*, what do you think of? Did you think Netflix? What about a swoosh? It's Nike, right? Surely you recognize a big yellow *M*—the McDonald's brand is everywhere!

What Is Branding?

Essentially, **branding is using symbols, images, slogans, and more to make your company recognizable in the marketplace.**

Branding can be a phrase, slogan, or song:

- Financially Simple: "Let's make our lives, at least, financially simple"
- Dave Ramsey: "Better than I deserve"
- McDonald's: "I'm Lovin' It"
- Subway: "Eat Fresh"
- Skittles: "Taste the Rainbow"

Branding can be a design:

- Target: red-and-white bull's-eye
- UPS: brown delivery trucks
- John Deere: green tractor
- Chick-fil-A: mischievous black-and-white cows
- Domino's Pizza: red-and-blue domino, duh

Branding can be a reputation:

- TOMS: donates a pair of shoes for every pair sold
- Warby Parker: donates a pair of eyeglasses for each pair purchased; also trains people in developing countries to give basic eye exams
- BOGO Bowl: matches pet food purchases with donations to animal shelters
- Bombas: donates a pair of socks with every pair sold
- St. Jude Children's Research Hospital: reduces fees or offers free treatment for children

Branding can be a name:

- Bass Pro Shops
- NerdWallet
- Credit Karma
- The Truth About Money
- Financially Simple

We all recognize those names, slogans, and logos. More importantly, we often associate a feeling with those branding devices. You can almost taste the fries from McDonald's when you hear the "I'm Lovin' It" jingle. At McDonald's, all I want are the french fries. One time when I was in Malta, I wanted some McDonald's french fries, but I couldn't find a McDonald's. I had french fries at another restaurant, but they weren't the same. That's the power of branding.

I know that if I go to Chicago and get a pizza, it's going to be a deep-dish slice of heaven. Yet New York is going to deliver a thin-crust slice of heaven. I know if I'm at the little German lady's restaurant here in Kingston, Tennessee, not too far from my house, it is going to be the best pizza you've ever had this side of heaven. Branding is all about perception and expectation.

If a company has branded itself well, you know what to expect when you see its logo. You get excited when you see a box with the Amazon logo on your doorstep. It stands to reason that having an established brand is essential when building your businesses marketing campaigns.

Four Cs for Branding Your Small Business

If you understand the value of branding, then you know you ought to brand your business. But how do you go about branding your small business? Well, there are four Cs to branding. Branding must be

1. Consistent—be consistent in your delivery and message across every venue.

One of the things I look at when working with new clients is their branding. I'll often find that marketing is not consistent across multiple venues and mediums. The business card will look one way, the social media will look another way, and the website is typically all out of whack. There's no consistency in delivery, and there is no consistency in message. Take an inventory of your branding.

The brand might also be *you*. Gary Vaynerchuk, or Gary Vee, has done a nice job of that. The authors and speakers Grant Cardone and Ric Edelman, too. Everybody is creating brands for themselves these days. Your brand can be corporate, or it can be individual, but it has to be consistent.

2. Clear—make your brand easy to understand.

Apple's logo is an apple with a bite out of it. Netflix's logo is the letter *N*. Great branding is easily recognizable and easy to understand.

3. Concise—keep your message simple.

In 2018, the chain restaurant IHOP—International House of Pancakes—announced that it was adding burgers to the menu and changing its name to IHOB: International House of Burgers.[34] People panicked. It was all just a big stunt, but it confused the heck out of everyone.

4. Continual—place your message everywhere and anywhere you market.

Branding isn't just for one location; it's continual and nonstop. You are branding yourself and your company every day. Once you create a brand, proliferate your market with it. Put it on your social media sites, podcast sites, and websites. Include it on your business cards, emails, nameplates, vehicles, envelopes, stationery, and more. The more your targeted market sees your brand, the more they will remember your business. The more often they buy your goods and services, the more you will leave a positive impression in their minds.

How are you doing in your business? Do you have a consistent brand? Is it clear and concise? Are you branding continually?

Your Baby's Beautiful

Whenever we're dealing with growing your company's value, we're not talking about increasing the top-line revenue. We're talking about how we can raise the value that **somebody else would pay** for the company.

Entrepreneurs don't always see an immediate value or return on their marketing investments, so they think marketing's not worth it. But their shortsighted view can lead to long-term loss of revenue.

The Hot Dog Vendor

Few things in this world are as satisfying as a good hot dog. The possibilities for flavor combinations are endless. I like a West Virginia Dog with chili, onions, coleslaw, and a little bit of mustard. Aside from making myself hungry, this leads me to my next point about marketing.

I want to tell you a parable I heard about a hot dog vendor who operated a mobile cart in a major city. Every morning, Mark the hot dog vendor would go to his spot, and everybody knew where it was because the interstate was just above him. He'd purchased strategic billboard advertising right before the off-ramp of that interstate that said "Greatest hot dogs here," with an arrow pointing to his spot. Each day when Mark arrived at his spot, he would find patrons waiting to purchase his delicious hot dogs.

As the story goes, Mark's business continued to grow. Then a recession happened. Nonetheless, he was still selling hot dogs because people have to eat, even if they're out of work, and hot dogs are a fairly low-cost meal. But, fearful of what the recession might mean for his business, Mark decided that he needed to cut back and do what he could to save money. So, he quit paying for his billboard advertising. Before long, patrons ceased lining up before Mark arrived at his spot. Loyal customers continued frequenting his business for a time, but eventually, he lost his robust sales, and his company folded.

Are Your Marketing Efforts Working?

Although Mark's story may be a simplistic way to prove the point, it illustrates the vital role marketing plays within a small business. Real-world examples are not so obvious, so how do you know whether or not *your* marketing works?

First, you create a marketing budget based on the goals you've set during your strategic-planning sessions. Exactly how much money you should spend on marketing is up for debate. The Small Business Administration (SBA) recommends that businesses spend about 7 to 8 percent of their **gross revenue** on marketing on average. The SBA says that growing companies should spend between 12 to 20 percent and established companies should spend between 6 to 12 percent.[35] I think that the more you can allocate toward marketing, the better. I believe value maximization demands at least 20 percent of net income (after the cost of goods sold) allocated to marketing.

But before throwing money at the first marketing strategy that comes to mind, do A/B testing to decide which campaign will work best for your business. Determine which drives more traffic to your store or eyeballs to your site by **tagging** your actions. For example, some technologies create a forwarding phone number, enabling you to track leads that come in from specific advertising sources, or you can use QR codes or custom URLs to determine which advertising elements are bringing the most customers to you.

After you've done that, it's time to create a detailed plan for how you will spend your allocated advertising dollars. You will likely have high front-end costs to get your marketing going in the right direction. Maybe you have to pay significant fees to a website developer or a marketing company. But after those initial up-front costs, you need to know how and where you'll spend your monthly marketing budget.

Finally, you're going to quantify your marketing results. You'll track URLs, calls, sales, QR codes, etc., to see if the dollars you're spending are worth the results you're getting. Essentially, you're trying to determine your marketing cost per lead, sale, or customer you attained. Then, you'll look to see if your efforts increased sales.

Why Marketing Is Worth the Investment

Why is it that small-business owners think marketing is not worth the investment? It's because we are jacks-of-all-trades in our businesses. We try to be everything to our businesses and fulfill every role. But we eventually realize that's not an effective system. We don't have the search engine optimization or marketing knowledge we need to create and track marketing campaigns.

If you're trying to increase your company's value to sell it for profit or attract investors, you will need to be able to show how you've succeeded. A marketing budget and a marketing plan will help you drive up your company's intangible value by showing buyers or investors exactly what you've done and just **how beautiful your baby is**. You can show potential buyers what campaigns you've done and what advertising venues you've used. Then, you can quantify the results of your dollars spent and show potential buyers what worked. All this will show that you are a best-in-class company.

How Marketing Brings Value

The sample value-maximization process questions below can help you gauge your company's efforts in marketing and define areas of focus to help you achieve greater value. The process is covered in more detail in the book's conclusion.

Marketing Leaders

- Does your company have a true marketing director, or do they have multiple areas of responsibility?
- Is there a dedicated team tracking the company's marketing efforts?
- How is the marketing executive qualified for their role?
- How is the marketing team skilled in leveraging social media and web-based techniques?
- If your company is too small to focus on web-based technology, are you outsourcing your marketing to yield results?

Marketing means a lot more than just throwing mud against the wall or doing whatever your friend says.

Marketing System

- Is there a fully developed and documented marketing plan?
- Does that advertising strategy align with your business's overall plan, mission, and values?
- Has the company identified and defined a specific marketing target or persona?

Marketing system goes back to your business plan. If you don't have a business plan, not only are your sales and leadership weak, but your marketing is inefficient. The business plan is vital for so many things.

Market Analysis

- Have you implemented a process to pinpoint the strengths and weaknesses in your competitors' marketing efforts?
- Do you have a method for establishing the best pricing for products or services?
- Are there systems in place to actively track a client's experience?
- How successful is the company at delivering positive client experiences?

Market Analysis will help you determine if you need to adjust your branding.

Corporate Identity

- Is there clear and consistent branding across the entire organization?
- Does it match the goal and values of the company?
- Does the branding match and appeal to your target market?
- Is your internet presence (i.e., website, social media) generating leads, or is it just an internet business card?

Marketing Budget

- Is there a dedicated allocation of funds for marketing?
- Does this amount include the total cost of your marketing plans?
- Across the past five years, what trends are apparent in your marketing spending?
- Do your marketing strategies include metrics to track your return on investment (ROI)?

You shouldn't use your financial resources for marketing unless you know the return. Many people out there market, market, market, and throw dollars here, there, and everywhere only to end up wasting their money. Then they say marketing doesn't work, so they cut the marketing budget.

The Bottom Line

A fair amount of total revenue—as much as 20 percent in some industries—should be allocated to marketing. You may think that seems extreme, but if you're doing marketing right and you spend dollars correctly on branding, positioning, strategy, and team, then those dollars are going to return many times over. You're going to reap what you sow.

While growing corn in East Tennessee, we planted a bag full of seeds that only cost us $3. Soon, each kernel of corn we sowed had a stalk of corn with one, two, or sometimes three ears of corn. And each ear of corn has hundreds of kernels attached. We sowed the seeds, and we reaped much more than we planted. But it took time for us to reap.

In marketing, you have to deploy dollars, but you also have to track the spending and recognize the results, which is where so many businesses lose focus. They throw marketing dollars out and then don't track them, so they don't know the outcome of their spending. Then, whenever a buyer comes along, they say, "Oh, you need to cut your marketing. You're not using it efficiently." Well, no joke there! You didn't even track what you were spending on, so you can't project your sales. You can't work on your financial projections properly. You can't measure your marketing ROI. When you try to pitch your company, the buyer's going to say, "You don't have a clue what you're doing. You're just throwing dollars into the wind."

That inability to track your marketing efforts is going to cause your company's value to drop significantly. Marketing directly affects the company's value insofar as it's going to show the buyer exactly what you've done. You're going to receive a more significant market share as you become more efficient, which in turn increases your company's value.

Action Item: Marketing

Any successful marketing plan starts with analysis—a review of what's worked, what hasn't worked, market trends, and how those things connect to your overall business goals. That analysis will help you make smart choices and get the best bang for your buck when you spend your marketing dollars.

CHAPTER 6

Personnel: Who Will Help You Raise Your Baby?

What makes a great team?

It's easy to think of teamwork in terms of sports, where football teams like the University of Alabama's Crimson Tide always seem to rise to the occasion. Unless you're a solopreneur, you have team members who are vital to your business. Quite honestly, you probably can't run a successful business without your team. Every person has a unique personality, bringing a different set of positive and negative attributes to your business. So how do you get individual employees to work together like a well-oiled machine? All great employee teams have the same aspects in common.

Businesses that sell for the highest value are the ones that allow companies, venture capitalists, or strategic businesses to purchase them and have them independently generate a return for investors. Business owners, especially small-business owners, imagine an investor will want the same level of involvement as they do. That's not the case. The stronger your team and the better its diversity, the more value it brings to a purchaser. If it's solely reliant upon the business owner—what I call owner centrality—then the owner becomes a weak link.

What we'd rather have is a business that still operates when the owner is entirely removed. Businesses that operate without owner dependence yield the highest value. From a buyer's perspective, it's important to have a great team that's not centered upon one individual's abilities. A team approach can be replicated.

To apply an example from the Alabama Crimson Tide, consider the 2018 College Football Playoff National Championship. Alabama's star quarterback, Jalen Hurts, was benched at halftime, and backup quarterback Tua Tagovailoa came on and led the Crimson Tide to a 26–23 victory over Georgia.[36] A good team will have bench strength and won't need to rely on a single person to drive the company. You want that kind of depth in your business. The stronger your bench, the more value your company has.

There are 14 elements that go into making a great team:

1. They have common, clear, and defined goals.

To build a great employee team, each member needs to know what the group is trying to accomplish. We have a great blog about this on the Financially Simple website: financiallysimple.com/tactics-and-actions-how-to-implement-your-strategic-plans/. In terms of the University of Alabama, every player on the team recognizes the goal of winning the national championship, and they recruit some of the country's top high school players with that specific goal in mind.

2. Make sure team members understand your company's culture and values.

If your employee culture doesn't align with your values, realign it. I know several people who've served our great country in the military, including a close friend who served in the Marine Corps. He has told me about his bootcamp instructor's mission to make sure new recruits understood the Corps' culture and values. My friend would always say, "Justin, these people were going to be guarding your back on the battlefield. They had to make the Marines' values their ethos."

Culture and values are also crucial in business. You need to ensure that team members are not acting in a manner that undermines the company's core values. Suppose someone does operate outside of the company's culture and values. In that case, other team members must be willing to either inform you or correct any behavior that could make the proprietor and the business look bad.

3. Diversify.

The more diverse your team members are in age, gender, race, ethnicity, beliefs, and personality, the more collective thinking and problem-solving can be done. Diversity means bringing together people that reflect a range of viewpoints, perspectives, and education levels. Not everyone can be the pitcher! You need someone at first base, left field, and in the bullpen. Diversity makes the team stronger and more valuable.

4. Place employees in roles that match their skill sets.

Make sure employees are appropriately equipped for and passionate about their roles. In a team like the Crimson Tide, a tall, lightning-fast player with great hands will be lining up as a wide receiver, not as a center on the offensive line. That wouldn't make any sense. A wideout on the line would provide diminishing returns for your team. In business, just like football, every employee must be in a role to make the most of their talents. Far too often people are placed in roles that they're not equipped or are lacking the passion or personality for. Having a key employee in the wrong position could affect your company's performance.

5. Expect 100 percent effort from every team member.

Expect employees to keep other distractions at home when they're at work so they can give their all to your business. When I played soccer, I remember our coach saying, "Leave it on the field." Whenever your team members are out there on that field, they should show up every day ready to give their all to each challenge or opportunity that emerges. As the old saying goes, where you are, be there.

6. Hold team members personally accountable for team results.

Don't let employees play the blame game. Instead, hold all employees accountable for their actions and the team's performance as a whole. A team member might want to get paid more, and that's okay. Still, more pay generally comes with more responsibility, and they need to be willing to accept their share of the accountability and consequences when expectations aren't met. In football, when a team-oriented quarterback makes a bad pass and overthrows his target, you'll often see him pat his chest to tell his teammates, "My fault." Team members must be accountable for the results without shifting the blame or giving excuses.

7. Encourage mutual support.

Leave no room for showboating. Instead, encourage team members to support each other. My uncle served in the US Army and often reminisced about an event during basic training. They had to complete a muddy obstacle course, similar to Tough Mudder events held today. One particular obstacle required them to climb over a big wall with the help of their team members. Depending on the wall's height, there were two or three people boosting an individual to the top, who would then reach down and grab the person below them to pull them over. If one team member did not exert 100 percent of their energy, the entire team would suffer.

8. Open lines of communication.

Winning teams communicate transparently without hidden agendas. Remember, words can help, heal, hinder, harm, hurt, humiliate, and humble others. Words are the most potent gift ever received, and the most destructive weapon ever wielded. Be kind and open with one another from the top down.

9. Resolve conflict.

Winning employee teams also have conflict resolution that starts with a desire to understand rather than to be understood. Conflicts allowed to fester can fuel animosity and discontent among your team, but addressing and resolving conflicts can help reinforce values while also showing team members how valued they are.

10. Show respect.

Even though team members have different strengths and weaknesses, successful teams remain respectful of those differences. There's a lot of truth in Aretha Franklin's song "Respect." Although people may not always agree with each other's viewpoints, they should maintain mutual respect and try to see things from others' perspectives.

11. Support, challenge, and strengthen decision-making.

Remember, anything with two heads is a monster! Yes, ultimately, the boss is the boss. But in a good team, the boss encourages team members to challenge, support, and strengthen their decisions. Challenging a decision will allow team members to better understand the boss's thinking and reinforce the company's values.

12. Clearly define team organizational roles.

Make sure that you place team members in clearly defined roles that use their strengths. The star player and the benchwarmer should understand their roles and how their talents and abilities are helping the team succeed.

13. Place strong leaders.

As leadership author John Maxwell says, "Everything rises and falls on leadership."[37] So, place strong leaders in leadership roles. Strong leadership will help guide your team forward by reinforcing and instilling the right types of values.

14. Have fun.

Finally, have fun. Great teams know how to have fun, laugh, and reenergize each other. Leading your team and your business can be tiring, but having fun can keep you engaged, just like that feeling you get when you come back from vacation.

Is Your Employee Team Great?

So, fellow business owners, do you have a team like this? Do your team members (bosses, managers, and rank-and-file employees) know your mission? Do they support each other, communicate, and show respect? Is your team strong in a few of these areas but weak in others? What improvements can you make? As Helen Keller said during a 1913 speech in Philadelphia, "Alone, we can do so little, while together, we can do so much."[38] Additionally, the old proverb says, "Go fast, go alone; go far, go together."[39] It's time to set aside differences and egos. Now is the time to work together as a team to increase the intrinsic value of your company.

Meeting Your Employees' Needs

I remember my dad telling me something important: "Instead of loving people and using things, we too often mix it up. We end up loving things and using people to get where we need to go."

Our companies' cultures are driven from the top down, but how many entrepreneurs focus on meeting their employees' needs? Business owners often let stress, frustration, greed, anger, control, manipulation, or blame guide their actions toward their employees and then receive the same in return. Owners accidentally create a culture of fear and dysfunction instead of a safe, positive work environment. By understanding what motivates people, business owners can create the right company culture and increase their business's overall value.

According to professional services company Aon Hewitt, "the best companies to work for engender high levels of employee engagement and commitment because the leaders of these organizations focus on meeting employees' basic needs and satisfying their growth needs. They focus on helping their employees feel happy and fulfilled."[40]

That statement identifies two things that are very important when it comes to culture: **meeting employee needs** and giving them **growth opportunities**. We have to recognize that everyone, whether they're the boss or the janitor, has needs—being heard, feeling valued, and providing income for their families.

Employees want to live a certain lifestyle, but they also have the desire to grow. I know some people who do not want to grow and are content with where they are. But many employees do desire growth in their role, and your company culture should facilitate that.

What Exactly Is Company Culture?

According to the website The Balance Careers, "company culture is the personality of a company. It defines the environment in which employees work. Company culture includes a variety of elements, including work environment, company mission, value, ethics, expectations, and goals."[41] You are influencing your company's culture from the top down, or you are allowing employees to affect your culture from the bottom up, or both.

The Importance of Positive Company Culture

A company's culture can be positive or negative. It is a fact that the people who come into contact with your customers affect how they feel about your company. If you or your employees have negative attitudes, it can be a stain on your business. Conversely, if your team exudes a healthy and happy company environment, it will not be missed by your customers, vendors, or suppliers. These people will want to work with your business. How, then, do you build a culture that meets employee needs to such an extent that they want to think beyond themselves? How do you get them to take pride in both themselves and in your company? As well as meeting their basic needs, you need to meet their existential needs. Let me explain.

1. **Meet employees' basic needs.**

- **Provide employees with financial stability**—guarantee paychecks. Don't work in survival mode, where employees fear their paychecks bouncing. Provide them steady, regular, guaranteed pay that meets their personal financial needs.
- **Promote harmonious relationships.** Next, greet team members warmly and speak respectfully to them. Foster warm, cooperative relationships company-wide and create something great for

employees to be a part of.

- **Train employees to excel in and be proud of what they do**. Meet employees' needs for self-fulfillment by training them to become excellent at their jobs.

If employees' basic needs are met, they will be more likely to continue to work for your company. But you must meet more than their basic needs to instill a true sense of loyalty within your team members.

2. Meet employees' existential needs.

- **Renew and transform your employees**. Give your team members more than a paycheck. Help them see beyond themselves. Offer them a chance to improve their skills. Empower them to participate in company decision-making and goal setting.

- **Build an internal community**. Inspire employees' commitment to your company by sharing your vision and values with them. Give them a sense of purpose, fun, and team spirit.

- **Give employees a chance to make a difference**. Form strategic alliances with community organizations, congregations, sports teams, etc. so your team members can be a part of making a difference in your company's community.

- **Offer employees the chance to serve their communities**. Making alliances is one thing, but having the opportunity to serve is another. To meet the most deep-rooted of your employees' needs, give them a chance to serve others in their communities through your company's activities.

Toxic Culture Is a Barnacle on Your Company

As a business owner, it's easy to read studies about the importance of company culture and roll your eyes, shrug, or brush it aside. You can't find a line item for "feelings" on your company's budget. You look at all of the parts of your company that require attention and probably think, "When do I have time to worry about everybody's feelings?" I get it.

I grew up on the ocean. We had boats all around us—big shrimp boats that dropped nets in the water and pulled shrimp out of the estuary there on the southeast Georgia coast. The bottom of the shrimp boats, docks, and piers were all covered in barnacles—a type of crustacean that grows on just about everything in the ocean. They're pretty sharp, and if you're not careful around them, they'll cut you.

Barnacles may appear insignificant because they are so small relative to the 75-foot-long shrimp boats. But barnacles create drag and make it difficult for the ship to move through the water, and that slowing can have a massive impact over time. Beyond drag, eraser-sized barnacles can jam or obstruct or interfere with the rudder, preventing a boat from going in the right direction.

There are a few ways you can fix the problem. You can take the boat out of the water and scrape off dry barnacles, remove them by power washing the surface, or clean the boat while it's in the water. They become a bigger and bigger pain if you don't deal with them. The longer you leave them, the worse it gets.

Toxic culture is like a barnacle on the underside of your company, keeping you from transforming your company as quickly or directly as you'd like. Ultimately, you could end up spending more money maintaining the ship because you don't have the right efficiency within your culture.

Think about your current culture. Do your employees care only for their interests or think about the company's good when making decisions? Where does their loyalty lie? Do they work for a paycheck or something higher than their own needs?

What about you? Are you so worried about personal financial gain that you're ignoring the financial needs of your employees? Are you in business for yourself without considering taking care of your team members' basic human needs? Do you concern yourself with employee retention and longevity, or do you expect employees to act in their own best interests? Is your company full of fear, dysfunction, and negativity, or is it full of harmony, service, and positivity?

Grow Your Great Employees

In her book *Growing Great Employees*, Erika Andersen relates the art of growing employees to gardening.[42] I love the idea of growing things—doing some hard manual labor, then watching God's miraculous power grow some crazy plants.

Growing starts with the soil. If your soil is trash or you don't have the right pH levels, the plant will probably not grow very well. I had that issue with blueberries, which require acidic soil. The soil on my farm is not very acidic. I have to amend the soil by adding items that increase its acidity—typically pine bark, oak leaves, or pine needles. On the other hand, green beans grow like weeds on my farm because the soil is perfectly positioned for that plant's needs.

The culture of your company is akin to soil quality—it's what allows things to grow. Factors like weather can contribute to growing conditions. Maybe you have lots of rain, or perhaps it's dry. Maybe your company flourishes in a great economy or wilts under negative economic influences.

You have chosen people who are an excellent fit for your company. Now is the time to take them to the next level by investing in them through training and professional growth. This commitment will give your employees opportunities to develop their skills and compound the company culture you are working so hard to build. Below is my list of 12 ideas on how to invest in employees, which can help increase your business's overall value.

Ideas for Investing in Your Employees

1. Ask questions about their professional path.

The first way you can invest in your employees is to seek to understand them. What do they want to accomplish in this job? Do they see it as a stepping-stone? If you're trying to grow your company's value, you may not want employees who are going to be here today and gone tomorrow. Instead, you want team members who are going to come alongside you and seek internal advancement. These employees want advancement in compensation, responsibilities, and duties, so ask about their employment goals, and show them ways to advance within your company.

2. Encourage professional development.

Whenever you bring employees into your team, you want to provide them with educational opportunities. Frequently help them enhance their knowledge base; don't let them settle for the status quo or lackluster performances. Teach them new things, or send them to conferences, seminars, and training sessions. Motivate them by giving them proper guidance in their profession and by offering them continuing education opportunities. By doing that, you can grow the future leaders of your organization.

3. Create a development plan.

If you're encouraging professional development, you must have a development plan for each of your team members. Develop a plan for individuals to progress within your company based on their professional goals. Show them where they can get to within your company. Encourage them to set their own goals as well as outlining your expectations for them. That way you know what type of professional development they need.

4. Turn your weekly meetings into educational meetings.

Teach your employees something valuable each week. If you're following these steps, you know your employees' goals, and you know what it will take to help them reach those goals. Give them valuable education in small bits each week. If some team members have knowledge that the whole team could use, you can have them teach others.

5. Pair your team members with mentors.

When you're training employees, you want them to receive a valuable education in-house as well as at other professional development venues. Besides educating them in weekly meetings, you can pair your newer team members with seasoned mentors. Or, if you're training a seasoned employee to move upward in your company, have a manager or supervisor mentor that employee.

6. Consider job shadowing.

Besides pairing mentors and mentees, you can have employees shadow other players within your organization. If you have someone who wants to move up into management, have that person shadow a manager. Shadowing goes beyond mentoring because it involves a team member watching another for some time to learn specific skills.

7. Delegate.

Additionally, you must delegate authority to your employees. You can't do everything yourself. Micromanaging doesn't allow your team members to grow and develop their own skill sets, so you must delegate jobs, positions, and leadership to give yourself more time *and* your employees a chance to learn and grow.

8. Give team members assignments that stretch their abilities.

As you're delegating tasks to your team members, give them assignments that stretch their abilities. Don't just give them menial tasks to keep them occupied; ask them to do difficult things. If they don't push themselves, they'll never reach the goals they have within your company.

9. Show your employees that you trust them.

Perhaps the most challenging thing for business owners to do is trust employees with their baby, but you have to trust them to do the jobs you've given them. Trust their life experiences. Trust their education and knowledge. Step back and let them do their jobs.

10. Help your team members build networks.

The 10th thing you can do to invest in your team members is to help them build networks. Besides assisting them in growing their opportunities inside your organization, help them build opportunities outside of it. You're not building their networks so they can leave your company; you're building them so they can bring in more business and build strong connections that will help them improve your company.

11. Be willing to spend money.

Obviously, if you're encouraging team members to participate in professional development—continuing education, training, and networking—you're going to have to spend some money. Giving employees the tools they need costs money, and if you're not willing to spend it, it's unlikely that your employees will get the tools they need on their own.

12. Ask for honest feedback.

Finally, ask your team members for honest feedback—and receive it without getting your feelings hurt. Just because you're the boss, it doesn't mean you know everything. You don't have all the answers. Ask employees what you can do for them. Ask them how you can help them grow professionally within your company.

Remember, your job is to serve your team members. You're trying to fulfill more than their basic needs. You want to help them fulfill their existential needs and care more about the company than they do about a paycheck. To do that, you've got to invest in your employees. You've got to invest time, money, effort, energy, and education in them. Treat them as team members, not as employees. J. Willard Marriott, whose hospitality company, Marriott Corporation, started with a root beer stand and grew to restaurants and hotels, often said, "Take care of associates, and they'll take care of your customers."[43]

How to Stop the Revolving Door

If there's one complaint I hear more than any other from business owners, it's that they can't keep employees. They go through the hiring process, find what appears to be a qualified team member, and bring them on only to have them leave within a short period of time. Sometimes life events happen that are out of your control, but people often leave a company for other reasons. If you're trying to grow an organization, having continuity and regularity within your team is vital. You need to jam up that revolving door.

I've seen clients who are always having to hire somebody new. Either they don't pay people enough or they treat their team members poorly. Their culture is awful. They don't respect others or delegate properly. They don't trust or train. But you can be different.

Let employees know what you expect of them and what they can expect from you. Ever-changing expectations can create undue stress on employees. I'm guilty of this at times—I come up with harebrained ideas and share them with my team, but they realize by now that it's just Justin blowing air. In the early days, though, my team would think these ideas were actionable items. Sometimes those ideas were worth doing, but sometimes they weren't. And me expressing them changed expectations and put added stress on my employees. I've worked to make my expectations clearer.

I also make sure to show respect to team members. That doesn't mean you have to yield to outrageous demands or insubordination! Respect means valuing team members' advice even if it sounds silly or unrealistic to you. It means taking the time to talk through conflicts and issues.

Give people multiple reasons to stay with your company using the following employee retention ideas.

Employee Retention Ideas

1. Trust is key.

Show your team members you trust them by giving them responsibilities that allow them to grow and gain new skills. Help them reach the next rung on your company's ladder. If opportunities emerge, look within before bringing someone in from outside. Provide employees with opportunities for advancement instead of giving them reasons to look to your competitors for more money, better titles, or greater opportunities.

People often leave companies because of managers, supervisors, business owners, and others in charge, not because of their peers. Have your managers mentor team members and let aspiring team members shadow managers.

2. Set a coaching culture.

If you continually berate team members about doing their jobs poorly but never provide any other feedback, you will lose your employees. Hold quarterly or semiannual reviews where you begin with positive feedback about what team members are doing right, then transition into what they can do better. But remember—coach them. Don't just tell them what they're doing right or wrong. Give examples and then help them develop plans to increase or improve performance.

3. Show appreciation.

I realize how crazy and simple this sounds, but don't forget to show your team members appreciation. It works. You should reward your team members by speaking well of them, complimenting them, giving them increased compensation, or doing other small things that make them feel appreciated. All team members make sacrifices to be at work, so show them you appreciate what they do for your business.

Another way you can show appreciation is by giving team members needed time off. Sure, you probably have a set number of sick days or personal days in people's contracts but go beyond that if necessary. Give them bereavement days, mental health days, or recouperation days periodically if they need them. Be as fair with days off as possible without putting your business in financial jeopardy.

If you have limited results with these options for retention in your organization, then take out the "golden handcuffs." If you want employees to stay, provide a comprehensive benefits package to help them and their families. Make it difficult for them to find anything better by providing the best yourself. Be forewarned: this option can add monetary risk, as the cost of providing benefits is often volatile and uncontrollable. Ensure employees stay with you a certain amount of time before they can access their benefits or have team members sign noncompete or nonsolicitation agreements.

Performance Management: A Mindset and a Process

Performance management is a mindset. It's an ongoing process of setting expectations early and clearly that starts as soon as you hire new team members in your organization. It's a process that helps supervisors and employees reach a shared understanding of what is expected in terms of behavior, results, and feedback.

Raising your baby is all about giving feedback to encourage them as they grow. When you see your baby doing something wrong, you calmly but firmly teach them the right way. And when they do something correctly, you encourage and reward them. You have a system in place for their eating, bathing, and bedtime, and you follow through on that system until it's second nature. Constructive feedback and affirmation show your baby that you're caring, present, and attentive.

Before you can conduct employee performance reviews, you must institute a performance-management system. If you're throwing employees into a semiannual or annual performance review without giving them the tools they need to be successful, then you're crippling them. You're also crippling your business.

Performance management is a process. It's not a once-a-year meeting. Performance management is preparing team members to meet their goals throughout the year. It's purposefully directing their actions without micromanaging them. How do you do that?

I recommend the following seven strategies:

1. Have clear, documented expectations of employees in their job descriptions and employee handbooks.
2. Regularly discuss the critical components of employment and corporate goals with team members.
3. Meet with your team members regularly.
4. Get 360-degree feedback about employees from other team members.
5. Share the performance-review criteria and meeting format with team members.
6. Work with team members to set individual and corporate goals.
7. Review both negative *and* positive things team members are doing.

Whenever we meet with a business client who's trying to understand how to set up employee relationships, we help them create a process.

We often have the employees write out their yearly goals by asking them open-ended questions. For example, "Sally, what specifically do you want to accomplish this year? Why is this goal important to you? If you meet this goal, will it help you reach your five-year career goals? Where do you see yourself in a few years?" Then we critique the goals and make sure the employees' goals align with the business's goals.

I love to do this at the beginning of the year because it's a time when everybody is in the mindset of setting goals. It allows the individual employee to align themselves with the overarching goal of the business. You may bring in the employee and say, "I see where you're going with this particular goal, but how can your goal help achieve the company's targets?" If you can get the individual employee to think that the goals are their idea, you'll have 100 percent buy-in to your company's aims.

In June, July, or August, we typically review. "Let's see how we've progressed toward our annual goal." It's important to hold employees accountable for the goals they set for themselves, which also align with the company's goals. One way to accomplish accountability is through a midyear meeting.

You will see what they've accomplished at the end of the year, and you'll assess them based on how well they've achieved their goals. This process can get interesting, especially if you're dealing with family, friends, or longtime employees, so you're going to have to use many communication skills and tact. The first time you do this, it might feel frustrating or somewhat silly. But as you begin this process and allow employees to work through their own goals, you can accomplish so much more in your business.

What I've shown is how to set expectations for employees. It's a seven-step process, and it's ongoing. Many business owners don't do performance reviews, and if they do, they just drag employees into their offices once a year for a stressful meeting. That's not fair to your team members. Let them know what you expect of them, and keep them up to date on where they stand throughout the year. You can make these mini performance reviews part of your daily routine; that way, employees aren't left wondering whether or not they're meeting your expectations.

Why You Need to Learn to Embrace Performance Reviews

Continually setting employee performance expectations is part of an ongoing routine that will contribute to employee growth. You should observe your team members throughout the year and provide feedback in incremental portions. About twice a year, you want to **formalize** the performance-management process by conducting a performance review.

Unlike the continual performance-management process, the performance review is a dedicated time when everything else stops so that no one gets sidetracked. It's a time for summarizing and formally documenting employee performance. The performance review is a time for employee engagement too, when they give and receive feedback.

Why Should You Conduct a Performance Review?

Bosses and employees alike generally dislike the performance-review process. Bosses might stop doing performance reviews because they feel they are a waste of time. Employees might be frustrated that they don't get performance reviews, their reviews are late, or they miss out on raises because they receive reviews that devalue their input or feel like box checking.

Or you might think, "Why would you need to conduct a performance review if you're actively engaging in performance management throughout the year? What purpose does it serve?" Performance reviews clearly explain to employees how they're doing and what they gain from meeting individual and corporate expectations. Essentially, the formal review process reinforces your expectations both for your employees and for the organization as a whole.

A performance review:

- gives an opportunity for formal, written feedback and dialogue about team member development,
- emphasizes or builds a culture of performance,
- reinforces expectations among team members,

- recognizes individual and corporate achievements,
- generates documentation and records, and
- justifies your employment decisions.

How Should You Prepare for the Performance-Review Meeting?

Before you jump straight into the formal evaluation, you should prepare for the meeting.

- Schedule the performance review in advance.
- Allow 15–45 minutes with each team member.
- Review the notes you've been taking on team members throughout the year.
- Have examples, outlines, and suggestions for how employees can improve.
- Start with your best performers to hone your skills and craft your meeting process.

Tips for Conducting a Performance Review

- **Don't allow any interruptions.** Turn phones off and block off your calendars so no colleagues disturb you during the meeting.
- **Open with pleasantries.** Be kind. Don't create a hostile environment.
- **Explain the purpose of the meeting.** Remind team members that the review is a mutual process.
- **Allow employees to assess their performance first.** Ask them open-ended questions about how they think they have performed throughout the year.
- **Review your appraisal.** Assess your employees' actions, behaviors, activities, and progress. Give specific examples to support your conclusions. Determine and document whether employees agree or disagree with your appraisal.

- **Develop a process for employees' next steps.** Either create a process that helps them reach new expectations or begin the process of termination.

Rate each employee's performance. Give them ranks, like platinum, gold, silver, or bronze, or give them grades, like exceeds expectations, meets expectations, or fails to meet expectations. Document everything as you go through the performance review. Go in with clear goals and expectations and place employees in positions where they can flourish, whether that's within your company or elsewhere.

The whole idea behind performance evaluations is to determine which team members perform at the level that will create the most significant possible value for your company. Top performers bring higher value to your business. That's just the way it goes.

Value

The systems and processes you build are ways to help a buyer see value in your company. Your efforts are enhancing the company's intrinsic value.

To return to the Alabama Crimson Tide again, head coach Nick Saban talked about his interview process. I was intrigued to learn that he follows very specific steps when recruiting and coaching.[44] For many business owners, we think we have procedures in place, but in reality, we are flying by the seat of our pants. I want to give you processes to drive up your organization's maximum value.

Saban discusses recruiting players four years ahead of time. He tries to recruit top players when they're in their freshman or sophomore years of high school. He identifies the type of person he's going to need for each position. You should do the same thing and gauge early how someone could contribute to your company.

To do this, you need to let the public know you're hiring. You may do this through an internal memo, social media, a hiring company like Monster.com, or even a headhunter. Once you receive applications, you have to narrow them down using a vetting process. If you get dozens or hundreds of applicants, how do you pick the top five? How do you choose the right person?

When you finally make a hiring decision, who's going to meet with the employee? Who's going to make sure they fill out all the necessary paperwork? Your HR department can help with this step. There should be onboarding and training processes in place to ensure a smooth start to their employment experience.

You may be a small company with only 10 employees, but they can be either 10 headaches or 10 opportunities. If you're trying to build a company for value, your system needs to be written out, formatted, and standardized to the point where any other business owner could walk in and implement your processes on day one.

You need a performance and education process. Your team's training can be in clinical training, informal training with team members, or in a formal classroom setting. How are you going to bring your team to the next level? You are preparing your team to be formally tested every year, just as Nick Saban is training his team to win yearly national championships.

You also need to work on your recognition process. We demand a lot out of our team. We all do. You might have some stellar performers and some not-so-stellar performers. You need to recognize and celebrate your top performers with incentives like bonuses, promotions, and perks. It could even be an extra day off.

You should formalize the advancement process, which is the way people move up in your company. You should identify the people you need in management and then vet and narrow the scope. Then you should onboard them into their new position and start training them.

The advancement process is similar to the hiring process, but you have to be careful because you shouldn't give a title change without extra compensation or advancement. Avoid lateral changes when the team member has more responsibility with less pay or a different job with the same pay because that can be demoralizing for employees.

And Then There's the Firing Process …

I'm not a fan of firing people. I don't think anybody is. It costs a lot of money and causes conflict within the team. Other employees might gossip or question the decision. That being said, you need a process. Whenever you have to fire someone, you should focus on conflict resolution with both the terminated employee and the remaining team. Defaming them could lead to a lawsuit.

We've seen organizations in the publicly traded arena where the board of directors or the CEO was fired. Man, that has a ripple effect on the equity position or the stock price of the company. Don't think for a minute that your small business is not susceptible to the same thing. If you don't handle the firing process well, you could face consequences with your remaining team members, the community, your customer base, and ultimately yourself. When I have to fire someone, I have trouble sleeping before and after. It takes an emotional toll.

Retirement Process

Some different rules and benefits come into play when someone legally retires. How are you going to handle it? Are you going to congratulate them? Will you provide them with a token? For example, my dad received a watch as a retirement token from his long-term employer. What are you going to do when your employees retire?

These processes are vital. Having them in place will help you drive up the value of your company. When a buyer comes in, they're going to wonder how you operate as a company, and the processes in place add intrinsic value.

How Personnel Bring Value

The sample value-maximization process questions below can help you gauge your company's efforts in personnel and define areas of focus to help you achieve greater value. The process is covered in more detail in the book's conclusion.

Human Resource Infrastructure

- Is there a true human resources officer, or is this handled in addition to other responsibilities of your management team?

- Does your company have a human resources manual? Has it been reviewed by an attorney?
- Do you have a documented structural chart? Has it been shared with the team?
- Are the responsibilities clearly outlined for each role and position in your company?
- Do all levels of employment throughout the company have equal access to human resources?
- Is there a standardized onboarding process for new employees?

People are vital to any company that hopes to transition or sell. Business owners today often make themselves the epicenter of the business. I'm guilty of this action myself. However, to increase the value of your business, you must end this habit.

Individuals will make or break your team. A team relies on every member. There are always stars on football teams, but candidly, even the best wide receiver, quarterback, or running back would be nothing without a dynamic line that protects them.

While these protections cover the legal side of hiring and firing (which I'll cover later in chapter 9), they also help establish stability and continuity among your workforce.

Personnel System

- Do you have a formally documented human capital strategy?
- Have you structured your hiring and personnel strategies to adhere to your plan, mission, and vision?
- Are there calculated plans to help you carry out the strategy?
- Does your company have systematized processes for hiring, interviewing, and performance-review?

- Do the performance reviews include everyone in the company? Are these reviews conducted in 360 degrees, meaning a supervisor and their peers are reviewing each other?

I regularly see business owners hiring people that are just like themselves, and that lack of balance allows blind spots to emerge. The company might be lacking something without diversity in its personnel. Creating a hiring strategy will help you systematically build needed diversity into your team.

Supplemental Training

- Does your company have a prescribed training plan for employees?
- Is reimbursement offered for continuing education?
- Is continuous learning encouraged or incentivized? It's been said that investment in learning pays the best interest. You need to continually train your team and give them every opportunity to learn new skills.

Bonus and Incentives

- Does the company have a formal employee-recognition program?
- Is there a structured employee-incentive program?
- Does your company seek new opportunities for the talent within its ranks?
- Is your company's compensation in line with comparable business's in your industry?
- Do you know the compensation and benefits for the market in which your business operates?

As business owners, we want to treat our team members well. But we often don't know how to figure out a bonus structure. Start by thinking about each person as an individual. You must keep in mind that not everybody's motivated by money; some are motivated by recognition or time off. Whatever the incentive, you want to motivate people and show them that you recognize their effort.

Identify and refine an incentive program that will unify the team. One of the things we're working on in our organization is equity participation. There's an old scripture that says, "For where your treasure is, there your heart will be also."[45] If you have equity participation within the organization, the team members genuinely want to see the organization grow because it will directly affect their financial status.

Scalability

- How long do employees stay at your company? Is your turnover rate higher or lower than your industry average?
- Are your employees being developed for the next level?
- Is there a standardized process to develop desired results?
- Is your process connected to sales, marketing, and operational functions?
- Does that process include avenues of feedback for quality control?
- What kind of system is in place to recruit, train, and retain a high-quality workforce?

If your employees have job satisfaction and have developed their knowledge base and skills, then you will have retention. Your personnel are genuinely invested in your business, and that passion, trust, and steadiness help your ability to scale. Continuity of team members prevents the old "two steps forward, one step back" scenario.

The Bottom Line

Personnel is often overlooked in terms of value maximization, but being able to hire, mentor, train, and retain the right employees reflects a robust system.

It's crucial to ensure that employees continuously improve and be given chances to succeed, and their efforts should be quantifiable and trackable. Whenever you invest in your team, that team will invest in your company and ultimately position it for success. When a buyer sees that, they know you have your own dream team, which will help you grow your company's value.

Action Item: Personnel

As your company continues to grow, your personnel's needs may change, and retraining may become necessary to prepare employees for new roles. Is the solution to your staffing gap already on your team? Don't be afraid to ask what employees want out of their careers and consider how they could match the company's needs.

CHAPTER 7

Operations: Make Your Baby Beautiful

I f you're trying to increase your company's value, you must build **business operational systems**.

I'm talking about the flow of your business—the way you deliver your goods or services to your customers. According to Investopedia, operations management is "the administration of business practices to create the highest level of efficiency possible with an organization. It is concerned with converting materials and labor into goods or services as effectively as possible to maximize the profit of an organization. Operation-management teams attempt to balance cost with revenue to achieve the highest net operating profit possible."[46]

Operations departments exist to create systems within every department that will maximize your business's profitability. For many small-business owners, though, having an operations department seems like a pipe dream. Even with a small staff, creating operational systems is a realistic goal. The systems are designed to help the company operate efficiently while preserving the **quality of the service's integrity.**

The more efficiently your operations department operates, the more profit the company usually experiences. Think about a water hose that has lots of kinks; it's not going to have a lot of flow. But if you straighten out the hose and make it go downhill, it will transport a lot more water. It becomes more efficient. It's getting the maximum amount of flow with the least amount of friction. Similarly, you can get the maximum amount of profit at the least amount of cost.

10 Things to Remember as You're Building Business Operational Systems

How do you improve your business operations or create effective operational systems? Well, you must keep the following 10 things in mind.

1. Operations include both people and processes.
2. Salaries and wages are often the largest expense of an organization.
3. People want to do good work.
4. There are very few quick fixes in the operations of an established business.
5. Business owners and leaders must systematize the processes that already exist in their heads.
6. Small wins build motivation, while large wins improve returns on investment (ROI).
7. Don't be afraid to ask for help.
8. Senior management only sees about 4 percent of the company's real problems. It's the iceberg effect, where business owners see symptoms of a problem rather than its source.
9. Operational systems help mitigate company risks.
10. Most of the time, you don't need to fix or improve technology.

You may think you don't have the time, resources, or money necessary to build an operations department. You might even say, "There's nothing wrong with the current system. It's doing its job." That's debatable. Maybe it is doing its job, but can you make the operating systems more efficient?

When it comes to operations, I want you to think **perfection.** Perfection in operations helps you create maximum flow through the business with the least number of restrictions. Whenever you vacillate about issues, it costs time and money.

Think about the water hose again. A water hose is easy to use and stays in better condition when it's wound up tight on a reel. Compare that to a hose that somebody wrapped up haphazardly on the ground; when you try to unwrap it, you have knots, wear and tear, and problems. Striving to build a tremendous customer experience through operational efficiency is monumental for both the customer and business. More efficiency means fewer headaches. All the pieces are working together.

Imagine if you had a car with a V-8 engine, but one of the cylinders didn't work, and the other seven cylinders were working overtime. You'd experience inefficiency, and engine problems could crop up. But if all cylinders were working correctly and doing what they should do, that motor would provide the optimum amount of horsepower.

By having business operations in place, you can build your business to a point where *you* are not necessary to its day-to-day function. You're never going to work *on* your business, rather than *in* it, if you fail to develop business workflows. You'll still be putting out fires years from now.

Establishing workflows will create a structure that allows your baby to thrive even when you're not present, which is the goal for any parent.

Work on Your Business, Not in Your Business

Having well-defined steps in business operations is a must, no matter how big or small the company. Even the smallest improvement to the management of a process will yield positive results. Since I work with more service-based businesses than manufacturing-based businesses, I want to give you the operational steps you need in place in your service-based business (note that a manufacturing business has many more steps).

As an owner of a small business, you tend to be the operational guru, or the chief operating officer, among the many other titles you carry. Your job is to provide a service to your customers, clients, or patients from start to finish. There are several steps your company and employees must take along the way. I want to go over the basic operational steps to make your job easier and your customers happier.

Operational Steps

1. Design and engineering

First, you need to design your offering. Determine what exactly you are giving your customers. Design and engineering are not just for manufacturing. Service-based businesses must also design their specific offering for their customer base.

2. Workflows for order taking

Next, you need to develop a workflow for what occurs when customers call and place an order for your service. Which team members answer the phone call? What do they say? What happens immediately after the phone call?

3. Project management

After receiving an order, what do you do next? Who will manage the project, and which team members need to help? What type of support will the team members need to fulfill the order?

4. Procurement

Formalize the relationship with the customer who placed the order. Develop a written agreement or an online agreement the customer will sign as an indication to begin work.

5. Resource management

Once the formal order is received, you need to gather and assess the materials and equipment you'll need to complete the work. Is the equipment you need operating efficiently? Is it in working order? Do you have all of the materials you need on hand, or do you need to order them?

6. Facilities management

You need a workflow to determine where and how you will store and maintain the materials and equipment you need for the order.

7. Technology management

As you're assembling the materials you need for the customer's order, what technology do you need to make the entire process faster? Are you able to take and send pictures for job approvals? What steps do your team members need to take with technology to make the work more systematic?

8. Team member management

Do you have enough staff to fulfill this order? What about this order combined with all of your current orders? Will you need employees to work overtime or hire new team members? Do you have the personnel you need to work efficiently?

9. Quality control management

How will you implement quality control when team members are working on the job? What can you do to ensure team members are doing their jobs? How do you reduce callbacks and complaints?

10. Sales management

While your team members are working on the current orders, who's out in the field trying to procure more orders? How will you ensure you'll have new orders once you complete the others?

11. Distribution

If you're selling a product along with your service, how will you distribute that product? What is the distribution process?

12. Packaging

How are you finalizing your service's provisions? How are you packaging your products? What will you do to demonstrate what you've done?

Be Like a Salmon

I love fishing, especially for trout. Here in East Tennessee, the Tennessee Valley Authority (TVA) and US Fish and Wildlife Service stock trout.[47] They put them into cold rivers beneath dams that are part of the TVA ecosystem and allow fly fishers to catch a few. Or, if you're like me, you might want to sink a Joe's Flies spinner or use a red hook with a worm.

One day, my brother and I went fishing on the Tennessee River, and we had a competition to see who would catch the most fish. I gave my brother the only red hook I had in my tackle box, and I used any color hook I wanted. It was as if I didn't even exist. I could cast the exact same type of worm into the stream, right beside my brother's bait, and the trout would hit his red hook over my shiny brass or gold hook every time. But I digress.

No doubt you've watched something on the Discovery Channel documenting the life cycle of a salmon. They begin life in a small river somewhere and then swim downstream to the ocean, where they spend most of their lives. They grow for five to nine years, depending on the species, until they near the end of their life.

A quest begins near the end of their life. They swim back up the river, against the current, to where they originally hatched to spawn. From September to November every year, adult salmon leave the ocean and swim upstream, jumping up waterfalls and trying to avoid bald eagles and bears that are waiting to grab lunch. These fish fight against all odds to swim up current.

The salmon run, as it's been called, is so vital to the ecosystems of the various estuaries and other bodies of water that there are mandates for its protection. On some dams you can find what's called a fish ladder. It's like a ladder that the fish can climb, and it allows the salmon to swim upstream without having to challenge the dam.

With that backdrop in mind, I want you to apply the salmon run to operations. Without solving problems, it's going to feel like you're helplessly swimming upstream. If the operational systems of your business are not working on adding value and growth to the company, you need to start looking for the cause of the problems. You may have to look long and hard. If you don't find the problem right away, keep at it. Most likely, you'll find that the root of your problems comes from one of **three operational issues**.

1. Inefficiencies in your operational processes

Go back to your operational processes. If you have no processes, that's your main problem. If you have processes, then look for inefficiencies, bottlenecks, or breakdowns.

2. Inconsistent execution of your operational processes

If your process structures are fine, the execution of the processes may cause your issues. How many exceptions to the rules are you or your team members allowing? How often are you deviating from your established systems? Try to understand what it is about that system that is causing people to want to deviate.

3. Excessive or unused capacity

If your processes and people are working seamlessly, the root of your problem boils down to capacity. You may be overstaffed or understaffed, have too much unused physical space or too little room in which to work, or your technological capacity could be strained.

If you have operational issues, you have infrastructure issues that could cause the foundations of your business to crumble. Look deeply into your business operations and fix the problems before they cause irreversible damage. As you're swimming upstream to find the source of your business problems, be like the salmon. Keep at it!

Keep Your Chicken Coop Clean

On our small hobby farm, we have 40–60 chickens at any given time. Taking care of this many chickens comes with great responsibilities but also teaching opportunities. Every day, the kids let the chickens out, collect the eggs, and throw some scratch feed. The chickens free-range on the farm all day long, and then when the sun goes down, they naturally go back to their roost, and the kids go back out and lock them up.

We also have to clean the chicken coop, which has its own process.

First, you have to get the chickens out of it. (Make sure it's not a wet, rainy day; the last thing you want is to have chicken poop on you when it's wet—it stinks!) We then open the doors to the chicken coop, pull the tractor in, grab all the waste, and put it over the garden or yard to use as fertilizer. Each of those steps has some key components: the tractor, tools, and new hay. We use diatomaceous earth powder inside the chicken coop, which doesn't hurt the chickens but helps keep the mites away.

Like farm life, there are different elements to the processes inside your business, regardless of which management system or operational system you want to use. There are **five elements that must be part of a good management system.**

1. Process and procedures

Let's deal with the process and procedures when hiring somebody. Your process should be thorough, proper, and streamlined, from the recruiting phase to the interview and hiring process to your new employee sitting at their desk on their first day.

Once everything is set, and you've gone through the final negotiations on the contract, the next step is the signing and start date. You have to create an email account and user profiles for the new hire. You have to create a workspace. Payroll, benefits, technology, etc. There are a lot of procedures.

2. Responsibilities within the organization

Weaknesses that emerge in a small business are often caused by trying to spin multiple plates at once. We've all seen that magic trick; that's how we may feel as a business owner!

Within the management system of your operation, who is responsible for every minor detail? When I was growing up, my mom would tell me, "Without responsibility, there can be no accountability." Since I was homeschooled, I got to hear sayings like this a lot. I am very grateful for that. Team members need to understand both their responsibilities and the penalties for not upholding the responsibility.

Many organizations outline their processes without defining responsibilities. You must teach the appropriate parties how they fit into the processes and procedures. That's a key element to an exemplary management system.

3. The right tools

Tools could mean technology, machinery templates, educational data, etc. Whatever the tool, your team members have to be equipped to succeed.

4. Minimize risk

Make sure you are doing everything you can to minimize the risks your team members encounter.

5. Matrix and reporting of processes

You should know how much output your operations will produce in a given day. How can you increase demand? How can you rise from the baseline capacity? How can you create more flow through the operations of your organization?

Suppose you take processes and procedures, roles and responsibilities, the tools, and the risk and safety controls and make those four elements paramount. In that case, you're now able to see where your company is currently operating and how much capacity you have before you have to increase scale. You can also design the frequency of the reports you receive hourly, daily, weekly, monthly, and annually. By tracking these metrics, you can find ways to become more efficient.

How Operations Bring Value

The sample value-maximization process questions below can help you gauge your company's efforts in operations and define areas of focus to help you achieve greater value. The process is covered in more detail in the book's conclusion.

Operations Leaders

- Does your company have an operations executive and support team?
- Does your support team understand the market?

- How has the operations executive been prepared for the role?
- Is the operations team equipped to endure transitional phases such as rapid growth, pivoting, or downsizing?

Operations are not just about efficiency. That's certainly part of it, but it's more about ensuring that your business is operationally sound so an investor will want to buy it.

I've often seen business owners who are experts at operations draw a premium for their business, all because of their best-in-class team. Build your team; grow your value!

Operating System

- Is there a documented and encyclopedic operating system, including operating policies and procedures?
- How are your mission and values supported by the system?
- Have you used tactical plans to identify the key performance indicators that will be monitored?
- Do the company's operating policies and procedures address all inherent risks?
- Are the systems built to accommodate future growth?

Having an operational system is vital. Have you written it down? Don't just read over this point! Let me ask you again: **Is your operational system written down?** I am making a big deal out of this because a buyer wants to see what processes you've implemented to create efficiency and improve your business. If you can show them what you've done, you've got something.

Think about how many businesses out there are operating based on the owner's mindset. Intentionally creating an operating system helps to download the owner's mind, allowing an outside investor to understand what steps were taken and what worked. It also brings awareness and clarity to the company's microscopic details, helping employees perform at their best, enhancing the customer experience, and letting the owner's mind rest.

You have to outline all your strategies, resources, assurances, and efficiencies in a manual. You want a process guide that shows *how* to do everything within the company.

When I'm coaching clients, I often have a conversation about vacuuming the floors. I usually begin with a question. "How do you vacuum the floor in your business?"

The client typically responds, "Well, I grab the vacuum and plug it in."

To which I respond, "Where is the vacuum located?"

"The closet" is a popular answer.

At this point, I typically ask a series of rhetorical questions like: "Well, in which closet do you store the vacuum? What's in the closet? Where do you keep the vacuum bags?"

You want your operations manual so detailed that somebody can look at any aspect of your business and make sense of it. It should be kept current and address any inherent risks.

Support

- What alternative resources are available if the company outsources?
- Have you created functions and disciplines for support services?
- Are internal support systems efficient?

Alternate resources can help your company scale up or down efficiently, and being nimble can be very appealing to buyers or investors.

Quality Control

- Is there a method to ensure quality within your company?
- What are your customer service practices?
- Are clients contacted each year? At regular intervals?
- How is overall customer contentment tracked and measured?
- Is there someone devoted to monitoring and enforcing quality standards within the business?

A healthy operations system means that someone besides the business owner can handle dissatisfied clients, so they are not at the business's epicenter. Operations will create a system that defines quality and tracks satisfaction to ensure that customers are interested in working with your company again. Assessments can identify performance lapses and focus on improvement.

Efficiency

- What are the company's efficiency initiatives?
- How frequently do errors occur? What percentage of projects involve cost overruns?
- Is the company attentive in exploring methods of uninterrupted improvement?
- Is there a process for when management should get involved?
- What is the annual revenue per employee?

If you can drive the annual revenue per employee up, you create a far more valuable business. Business owners focused on operational efficiency often excel in automation, team efficiency, and customer satisfaction.

Scalability

- Does the company have a high or low fixed-cost structure?
- Are there physical obstructions to expansion, such as a cramped office?
- How do vendor or subcontractor constraints challenge your ability to expand?
- What factors limit your company's recruiting efforts?
- Will the company have to relocate soon?

Identifying the barriers your company faces will help you recognize your strengths, difficulties, and opportunities and understand what is required to take on additional locations or contractors. It will make you sharper in your relationships with the people you're engaging. You will discover room for flexibility because everything is written down, documented, and straightforward. It's like having a playbook for growth.

The Bottom Line

If your operational structure is built to where the company can operate without you, then you've created greater value for your business. The only way you're going to get there is to identify the steps that the company takes—it takes years to do this, not just days. Your process must be written down, and you must test, improve, tweak, and refine it. Everybody must be on the same page.

Action Item: Operations

You want the company to be able to operate without you. Why not take a vacation? Leave instructions for your team and appoint team leaders to cover your tasks, then take a week away and don't check your phone or email regularly, except in an emergency. See what happens! See what works well and what doesn't, and when you get back, provide training or instructions to ensure that next time your team can cover any gaps that emerged.

CHAPTER 8

Finance: Predicting Your Baby's Path

I f you are trying to drive up your company's value, you must focus on reducing **risk**.

Value is interchangeable with sales price—your walkaway money, your "take this job and shove it" money. But no one is going to pay you for uncertainty. If you can't produce financial documentation that shows historical growth and projects realistic future growth, no one will be interested in buying or investing in your business. Or if they are, their offer will likely be insulting.

As you work on increasing the value of your business, I want you to pay close attention to the way you handle your company's finances. Let's find out how you're currently doing and what your company is capable of by considering the following questions:

- What financial information would you like to know that you are not getting today?

- Do you have a board of advisors or board of directors?
- Do you track sales and revenue through a financial management system?
- Have you created and prepared a budget for your business?
- Are you forecasting business growth through a pro forma financial statement?
- Are you using a budget and a pro forma to track your business's growth?
- Do you know what you need to do and when you need to do it throughout the year?
- Are you meeting with your professional advisory team from time to time to predict your tax bill and making the necessary adjustments?
- How are you managing your cash flow?
- Are you paying down your debts?

By answering these questions, you can determine how many improvements you need to make to your business's finance department. Precisely what are you missing? What are you failing to do? If you can pinpoint what you are doing wrong, you can develop strategies to fix the problems and strengthen your finance department.

As my *Certified Value Growth Advisor (CVGA) Handbook* says, a business's "value is influenced by risk and the predictability of future cash flows."[48]

Exactly **how can a finance department add value to your business?** Well, it can

- provide you with a financial analysis to improve performance and deliver consistent and predictable results,
- help you achieve the long-term goals you've created in your strategic-planning process,
- provide transparency to leaders and investors,
- create internal controls that reduce risk,
- maintain compliance with regulatory authorities to reduce risk, and

- manage cash flow to fund business growth.

Essentially, your finance department helps you track and predict revenue and profits, therefore mitigating your company's risks. The less risk your company faces, the more valuable it becomes to investors and buyers.

Why Every Business (Including Yours) Needs a Chief Financial Officer (CFO)

Many small-business owners can't afford a CFO. The cost—often more than $100,000 a year—causes some business owners to hire part-time CFOs to write reports and perform other tasks.

You might think, "Well, I already have a CPA, so why do I need a CFO?" Many times, certified public accounts become compliance experts and lose sight of the larger focus required of a CFO. Your company's financial needs involve more than taxes. You need a CFO to oversee multiple departments and to wear many hats within your organization. By creating harmony within the company's finance department, a CFO reduces your business's risk and increases its functionality.

If you're using your CPA for tax compliance and doing nothing else, you're putting your company at risk for financial problems. The person in charge of your company's fiscal wherewithal should be overseeing the following four departments in your organization:

Treasury. First, your CFO should oversee your company's cash flow, notably, its income, expenses, accounts receivable, and accounts payable. Additionally, the financial officer should monitor the investments, checking, and savings accounts.

Tax. Most obviously, your CFO should also oversee your federal, state, and local tax liabilities as well as your compliance with all tax regulations—a role that the CPA often fulfills.

Accounting. Additionally, your financial officer should manage account reconciliations, consolidations, and maintenance. This includes general ledger maintenance and account operations.

Finance. Finally, your CFO should be in charge of all financial reporting, planning, and analysis. This includes compliance with the Sarbanes-Oxley Act, which requires transparency and accuracy of financial reporting, if needed.

As the overseer of the four financial departments, the CFO fills four different roles in your organization. The financial advisory services firm Deloitte developed a framework for this called "The Four Faces of the CFO":[49]

1. **Strategist**. First, your CFO should focus on driving up company performance based on financial reports.
2. **Operator**. Next, he or she should work on company efficiency to increase profit margins.
3. **Steward**. Additionally, your CFO should help control company moneys and ensure they are not mismanaged or wasted.
4. **Catalyst**. Finally, the CFO should calculate, quantify, and execute the organization's financial plans.

Your company needs someone in charge of all financial departments—treasury, tax, accounting, and finance—who can act as a strategist, operator, steward, and catalyst. The CFO must be a balanced individual because it takes skill to drive up performance while increasing efficiency. Remember the DiSC assessment from earlier? A high *C* or moderate *S* personality is desired in this position.

If one person can't handle all four roles, then you need four different people to step into the roles and one person to oversee them. Maybe your CPA acts as your operator while your certified financial planner (CFP) acts as your strategist. Then, perhaps your board of directors becomes your company's steward, and the CFO becomes the catalyst.

You, as the owner, oversee all departments. Whether one person or five people handle your company's financial divisions and direction, your goal is to create an equilibrium where all departments function together. If they do not work together, you will miss compliance regulations, tax liabilities, general ledger issues, or reporting problems. By overseeing all financial divisions and making them work in harmony, the CFO reduces business risk.

HOW MUCH CASH TO STASH

PERSONAL	BUSINESS
CHECKING	CHECKING
1 MONTH OF LIVING EXPENSES	**1 MONTH** OF OPERATING EXPENSES
SAVINGS	SAVINGS
5-7 MONTHS OF LIVING EXPENSES	**2 MONTHS** OF OPERATING EXPENSES

How Much Cash Should You Stash?

Cash flow is the bread and butter of your business, but how much cash should you stash in your business and personal accounts?

Most of the time, I find that business owners forsake their personal finances to build their businesses. They are often operating their businesses to the detriment of their personal finances. As a result, I usually suggest that my business-owner clients use a four-account system to stabilize their financial situation and sustain their personal and business lives. In other words, they need to have two accounts for their personal cash flow and two accounts for their business cash flow.

I recognize this is an oversimplified process, but I think the four-account method is a smart system that you can apply to your own particular needs. Here's how it works:

1. Personal checking account

First, I recommend keeping the amount of money you and your family use monthly as a cushion in your personal checking account. For instance, if you and your family earn and spend approximately $5,000 each month, then you need to keep an ongoing balance of $5,000 in your checking account.

2. Personal savings account

Next, I generally recommend keeping five to seven months' worth of monthly cash flow in your personal savings account if you are a one-income family. If you are a two-income family, then you may only need four to six months' worth of cash in your emergency fund. If you make and use $5,000 each month, keep $20,000 to $35,000 in your personal savings account.

Having money set aside will help you make quick, prudent business choices whenever opportunities present themselves. Once your personal savings are in check, your stress level goes way down. I call it pillow money—the kind of money that will help you sleep easier at night.

Challenging circumstances will always emerge, but having enough money set aside will position you to make decisions at work without being affected on the home front. People often build their businesses but forsake their home and personal freedoms, and eventually, their business suffers too. Caring for the family first lets you focus on building your business accounts while having peace of mind that your personal finances are secure.

3. Business checking account

Now that you have your personal finances in check, you want to have the right amount in your business accounts. If your business income remains steady throughout the year, I typically recommend keeping your budget baseline in your business checking account. Like you did in your personal accounts, determine how much cash comes in and out of your business each month and keep *at least* that amount in your business checking account. If you earn and spend approximately $100,000 each month, keep $100,000 in your checking account funds.

If you work in a business whose income ebbs and flows according to seasons, I generally recommend keeping three times the amount of monthly cash flow in your checking account. If your expenses amount to $100,000 each month, keep a baseline of $300,000 in your business checking accounts to get you through the slow seasons.

4. Business savings account

Finally, I recommend keeping two months' worth of business expense necessities in a business savings account. These nonvolatile expenses could include basic utilities, rent, debt payments, employee payroll and liabilities, insurance premiums, and so forth. Traditionally, if you have two months' worth of necessary expenses set aside and you have stable income, then you can weather the worst storms when they come.

Too Much Cash

For years I have been preaching that business owners need to have cash and marketable securities, or "dry powder." The name is a callback to the days when warships would use gunpowder, which would need to be kept dry in case of a battle.

When I analyze business owners' cash positions, I often hear, "Justin, that too much cash! Shouldn't we deploy the extra cash to income-producing property, or a piece of equipment, or a beach house on Culebra?"

No! Cash is king. We often grow cash in times of great prosperity, but wealth is created in times of famine. The dry powder allows business owners to drive their business value during lean times while their competition is sucking wind. Think of cash as a boost of energy for the back half of a marathon. When you're at mile 20, you'll still be going, while others who exerted too much energy at the starting line are falling further and further behind you. We've seen this happen during the COVID-19 pandemic. We worked with businesses that kept extra cash on hand and were able to deploy it strategically, and it helped them dominate their competition and grow their business. Many companies that didn't set dry powder aside were forced to pull back or lay off or furlough some of their employees, and lots of businesses ended up closing.

An Exception to the Rule

I have yet to hear a business owner tell me that it doesn't provide peace to have cash in the bank, but there is one exception to the four-account method. If you are looking to sell your business in the next five years, then cash could be your enemy. At that point, you want to remove excess cash from your accounts in case buyers think you need that much cash to sustain your business, which could negatively affect your business's valuation.

Why You Should Stash Your Cash

The psychology behind this "cash stash" is amazing. I've worked with many business owners who struggled to reserve cash. Yet once they had "enough" in their personal and business accounts, their businesses began flourishing.

But why? The four-account method works because it reduces business owners' stress. With a security blanket in the bank, you have the ability to go out and take risks you weren't able to take before.

Keep the Cash Flowing In

Now that your cash is in order, it's time for the business to get paid.

More specifically, it's time to get paid in a regular, timely manner to build up your cash reserves. Your CFO or the department head in charge of your treasury oversees your cash flow, including your accounts receivable or administration and resource division, which is directly responsible for collecting customer payments. The finance department is directly responsible for the health and well-being of the cash flow into your business.

To keep the cash flow coming in, I have **19 tips** for improving accounts receivable collections.

1. Create relationships.

Build strong, healthy relationships with your customers, clients, or patients through a customer relationship management (CRM) system and social media. The closer you are to customers, the more likely they are to pay you. Marketing will help with this.

2. Use credit applications.

Set up a professional credit application for long-standing customers. If you approve customers' creditworthiness, have them sign a contract and use professional invoicing software to bill them.

3. Set credit limits.

Start by extending moderate terms to customers. Then, let them work their way to more flexible terms as they prove they can pay timely.

4. Create realistic payment plans.

As you offer credit terms to customers, make sure you don't overextend credit to them. You want to reward long-term customers, but you don't want to harm your cash flow by offering excessively lengthy payment plans.

5. Invoice immediately.

Start emailing or faxing customers copies of their bills. Expediting how quickly customers receive their bills can improve how quickly you receive customers' payments.

6. Update customer payment terms.

If you send invoices electronically, you can change terms from "due in 30 days" to "due upon receipt." Collecting receivables faster can revitalize your cash flow.

7. Update your billing cycle.

Besides updating payment terms, you can update your billing cycle. Rather than waiting to bill customers at the end of each month, bill them once their jobs are completed.

8. Anticipate early payments.

Once you send initial invoices, don't wait for customers to pay you late. Send friendly reminders through your CRM system or email to remind them of upcoming due dates.

9. Offer multiple payment options.

Offer your customers several different ways to pay their bills to make it more likely they will pay quickly.

10. Offer installment plans.

If customers are having trouble paying their bills and can't get approved for credit, then you might consider offering them in-house installment plans. Getting some money in small increments is preferable to getting no money.

11. Institute rewards and consequences.

Offering discounts or other incentives to customers who pay on time or early can increase your chances of getting paid quickly. Similarly, adding finance charges to customers' accounts when they fail to pay on time can push them to pay quickly.

12. Don't wait to collect.

Once you find out that a payment is late, don't wait. Contact the customer immediately to collect payment because it will be harder for you to collect the longer you wait.

13. Send reminder letters.

Some customers may not realize their payments are late. Therefore, constantly remind them that payments are due or late. A simple reminder letter may accomplish more than you realize.

14. Make a call.

If you've sent a reminder letter and had no response, pick up the phone and make a call. Be ready to offer multiple payment options and to accept payment there and then.

15. Don't get distracted by excuses.

Often when you make collections calls, you will hear excuses about why customers are not paying. Be prepared for those and require action from customers.

16. Be professional.

When you make contact with customers to remind them about late payments, you must stay professional. Hopefully, you'll see them again, so you don't want to say or do anything that could harm your relationship or keep them from buying your goods or services again.

17. Continue to treat customers with respect.

Remember that even the best people fall on hard times. Satisfied, long-term customers are a valuable asset to your company's revenue stream and cash flow, so don't hold grudges if people pay a little late, and ensure you continue to fulfill your obligations to them on time.

18. Up the ante.

It's okay to up the ante when necessary. If customers are not paying their bills and your finance team has reminded them, it's time to try something else. Consider reporting their late payments to credit bureaus, which will affect customers' credit scores, or call a debt-collection lawyer to help you take legal action.

19. Seek help from the experts.

If you're having multiple issues with late payments or delinquent accounts, don't be afraid to ask collection agencies to help with your accounts receivable.

Any and all of these tips can improve accounts receivable collections.

Trust me, just one of these tips may be the "tiny" issue you're having in your organization. Therefore, crack down. Get organized and get personal. Stay in contact with your customers, but stay professional. You have the power to improve the cash flow into your business. Take back that power today.

Streamline Your Accounts Payable Process

You hate paying bills. We all do.

I have a close friend who, when he receives a bill, jokingly says, "File 13!" and throws it in a special box to ignore it until the last possible moment. I wouldn't recommend that approach. It can wreck a company.

Conversely, some companies will prepay a significant amount to create credit with a potential supplier or vendor. A smooth, efficient accounts payable process will add value to your business.

It's not uncommon for a business owner to be untrusting. They're under constant attack. Attacks can come from employees, customers, the media, or even politicians these days—business owners are doing the best they can. But amid all this, business owners can become reclusive. They want to trust people, but it's difficult. The area where we see this most is the processing of money.

Conversely, having much trust in this area and not enough systems in place can lead to embezzlement. There was a dentist, whom I'll call Jordan, who was untrusting because a dear friend of hers had become a victim of embezzlement by an office manager. Jordan also had more competition moving into the area, and she found herself becoming suspicious of her team and dividing office tasks among its members.

The way we adapted her business to address her distrust while also improving her financial operating systems was by using automation. Don't overlook this point! If the owner, executive, or management in your business can produce $2,000 to $4,000 an hour, we must focus their efforts on the task yielding this result. Anything distracting an owner from the highest and best use of their abilities must be dealt with creatively. Automation and technology allow owners to oversee areas of distrust while not wasting valuable production time.

In this particular case, Jordan did not trust anybody for various reasons, but she knew she had to do something. She had the office manager and a process manager doing separate, disjointed tasks. It was tough to understand. Jordan found comfort in a system that integrated as much technology into that process as possible—from tracking when people came into the office to integrating payroll. Even having an external accountant who was able to check the books and follow the flow of money movement using a portal built trust for her. More importantly, we streamlined the system so that Jordan could get one report that gave her key metrics at the end of every week. We taught her how to read the metrics to identify if shenanigans were going on within the business.

We could move Jordan away from her fear mentality through automation and free up her time capacity to perform the $2,000-an-hour job that she trained and studied for years to do.

Uncover the Story of Your Company's P&L Statement

When I take the boat on the lake in the summertime, we pull the kids behind us on tubes, and I sway them a little bit to see if I can throw them off. As a boat cuts through the smooth Tennessee mountain lakes, it throws out a wake and prop wash. If you look back, you can see exactly where you've been.

Seeing that trail can be helpful, but you can't captain a boat looking backward. You have to continue to look ahead, watching for debris and other obstacles. For many companies, a profit and loss (P&L) or income statement is like that wake, no more than a trail showing where you've been.

Business owners typically look at their P&L statement at the end of the year. Although they may glance over it, most entrepreneurs consider P&L statements as something important to the "financial people." Most business owners don't know how to read the reports. If you are one of those business owners, then you are crippling your financial department. Without your P&L's story, you cannot create a transformative business budget, nor can you build a pro forma. So today, let me show you how to read a P&L statement.

If you are using bookkeeping software, you should be able to access your P&L statement fairly easily. Once you pull up the report, you can specify which dates you want to analyze. Typically, business owners or CPAs want to see monthly P&L statements or year-to-date P&L statements.

Revenue/Income Stream

At the top of your P&L statement, you'll see the income produced by your organization.

Typically, I ask business owners to **allocate their revenue stream according to the major income sources that come into the company**. For instance, if you own a swimming pool company, you might divide your revenue into construction, maintenance, repairs, store sales, etc. If you are a dentist, you might separate your services into preventive, restorative, cosmetic, etc. In a retail environment, you might divide your income into payment types like cash, checks, credit cards, financing contracts, etc. Or if you own an agricultural store (one of my favorite shopping destinations), you may divide the income into department types like hand tools, seed, fertilizer, plants, tractor parts, etc.

Essentially, you're looking for your revenue leaders. If you know what brings the most income into your business, you can develop marketing plans and budgets around it. But look closely at your P&L statement—**your revenue leader may not be your profit leader**.

Expenses

The next section of your P&L statement will involve losses, which are the expenses needed to operate the company. Those expenses could include the cost of goods (COGS), which typically include small equipment and supplies. For a pool company, COGS could include concrete, chemicals, and subcontractors. For an auto repair company, COGS could include parts like engines, transmissions, and brakes. Gross revenue minus COGS gives us gross profit.

The P&L will also include general business expenses like employee salaries, utilities, marketing, insurance, and rent—the expenses needed to run the company. If you look hard enough at your expenses, you might find some places to save money.

Doing the Math

Your revenues (profits) minus your expenses (losses) will reveal your net income.

All of those numbers will ultimately yield to a concept called "five by five by five." We want to try to see revenues increase by 5 percent, expenses decrease by 5 percent as a percentage of gross revenue, and our margins increase by 5 percent. If you can do that, major progress is being made.

Records Matter

You must maintain adequate records, year after year after year. If you don't keep good records, it's very tough to see where you have been and, more importantly, where you are going. If you're trying to drive value in your company, records can help you make real-time adjustments in the month, quarter, or year. Without the guidance financial records provide, it becomes increasingly tricky to project the glide path of your company's value and adjust to changing conditions.

And please, please stay up to date with your taxes, especially when you're trying to sell your company! A couple of years ago, I was working with a business owner to plan the sale of his business and build a lifelong income plan. His company was profitable, and he had worked hard to grow its intrinsic value. But he couldn't sell at the price he wanted because he hadn't paid all of his taxes. My client hadn't purposefully eluded tax payments. He just missed one, year after year. He had no idea it was due, and it ended up costing him the sale of his business.

If you don't pay your taxes on time, especially your payroll taxes, it could leave the buyers with a huge liability. I've seen businesses that didn't pay their company or corporate taxes, and there was such a significant tax burden and penalties for the stock sale that the buyer had to flip from a stock sale to an asset sale, and the seller didn't get nearly as much money.

Pro Forma

A pro forma shows us where we've been and where we're going. It's kind of like looking at a map while you plan a vacation and deciding between the various routes you can take to your destination. A pro forma shows how you're going to get there, how fast you'll need to drive, the stops along the way, and the expenses you'll incur. It's a mathematical projection into the future.

If you review past pro formas, things get interesting. By updating the pro forma every year, I can take my company back six, seven, eight, or nine years and see the projections for each of those years. I notice the years when I outperformed the pro forma and my company was doing better than what I projected. This matters when it comes time to sell the company. Part of the pitch book is going to reflect the company's potential going forward. If you can prove that you have systematically reached your positive growth objectives, then you're going to end up with a higher value.

With a pro forma, you're taking historical numbers from the last few years and trying to project them forward into the future. Your company's pro forma might go back five years, and you can use that data to project the next decade. If you're a mature business, your year-to-year growth might be 6 percent, but if your company is in its infancy, growth might double; I've seen businesses have 100 percent year-to-year growth in the early years. With your projections, you're making a hypothesis, a shot in the dark, a horseshoes-and-hand-grenades type of guess on your business's growth. Those projections will be based on historical performance as well as the best-educated guess you have.

Money In

You want your pro forma to outline where the money comes from. If you're an auto repair company, your pro forma could outline income from oil changes, engine repair, towing and hauling, loaner cars, and detail work. I have a pool-cleaning client who lists the income from concrete pools, fiberglass pools, vinyl pools, service and maintenance, repairs, storm damage—you get the idea. The pro forma should list various incomes so you can see, on a year-by-year basis, which division or area of the business is producing the most revenue.

The income portion of the pro forma should tell a story. You want to be able to look back and see which income sources are generating revenue. Those sources can all be totaled for gross income, which is a significant, bold number. You can then know that income is growing at a specific growth rate over the years and start extrapolating that growth rate over the coming years. Revenue is the fun part. It reflects your projections from your company's sales.

Money Out

Things get trickier with expenses because they can change at any time. Rent can increase. The market can tumble. You might need to make some emergency repairs on your building.

The easiest way to track expenses is through your P&L statements. When building a pro forma, consider downloading the list of categories from your accounting software—those might be advertising and marketing, accounting fees, rent, payroll, etc.—and under each of those categories, simply populate the expenses.

Say your accounting expenses were $8,000 last year. What are your accounting expenses going to be moving forward? You may run a simple inflationary increase of 5 percent, but if your income is expected to increase substantially, your accounting expenses may reflect that with a 15 percent year-to-year increase. Or your accounting expenses may stay the same.

With business insurance, you might see a pattern that your business insurance expenses are increasing about 15 percent each year. If those expenses were $13,000 at a point in time, then the next year they were $15,000, then $17,250, you can project a 15 percent year-to-year increase in that expense. That's not saying it always will increase 15 percent, but it's a safe assumption and an educated guess. You can build out these projections for every line item.

Looking Back, Looking Forward

The projections on your pro forma are reasonable expectations based on where your company has been and where you expect it to go. After you've run all of the numbers, you can show your total expenses and net income, which is your total income minus total expenses.

Some years your net income will wind up being a negative number, and that's okay. Some years will be leaner than others, and that negative number may correspond with some strategic moves you've made within the business. For example, moving the office will involve additional expenses making things lean from a cash flow standpoint.

How a Pro Forma Adds Value

With a pro forma you're ultimately tracking your margin—the degree to which your company is making money. Some organizations will have a marginal rate of about 30 percent, but some fields, like dentistry, will hit 40 percent or 50 percent margins. That is exceptional.

A pro forma can help you show numerically how you reached your margin, and that in turn means **you'll be able to ask a premium for the company.** I have built two different valuation methods into my pro forma. I have a value calculated using an industry-standard multiple. I also have an appraisal based on discounted cash flow methodology, so I know every year what my business value can grow to based on either metric. Building this can seem daunting. Visit FinanciallySimple.com/pro/ to see an example of a pro forma and learn how to build your own.

Now here's where it gets fun. I can look back, and I can see that my company was worth X three or four years ago, and I can see a rough estimate of what it's worth today. Whenever it comes time for me to look forward to the future, I realize that today's sacrifices are building up equity tomorrow. I realize that whenever I hire somebody, it's strategic. It's a direct equity play.

If I want to bring in a partner at some point, I have a direct model that shows where the company's value has increased or decreased over the years. Your pro forma is extremely valuable because it allows you to read numerically what's happened in your organization. It will enable you to see your net profit side by side, year to year. It allows you to track your organization's value, but even more than that, it allows you to maintain continuity with your key employees.

Teamwork Makes the Dream Work

Don't be afraid to show your numbers to your team! I make sure to hide individual payroll numbers but still put salary and wages together so my team can see the numbers of the company. I must say, whenever the group considers the organization's numbers, it results in greater buy-in. They understand the stakes, and they recognize that we're in this together. Did we hit our goal? Did we meet or exceed expectations?

In January, when it's time for us to talk about bonus structures as a team, we're now able to build a bonus structure in which we're all motivated. Everyone is motivated to drive maximum efficiency within the organization.

A Road Map for the Future

Whenever a buyer in the future looks at your data points, they'll want to see how you accomplished your goals and what you think the company is worth. They'll want to know that your company is truly going from X to Y and that it's not some phony-baloney you pulled out of thin air.

Suppose you want to increase your company's value. In that case, you must know where to spend money, cut money, hire people, fire people, use technology, or calculate a hurdle rate (the minimum acceptable rate of return). All those things come from the information a pro forma provides.

How Finance Brings Value

The sample value-maximization process questions below can help you gauge your company's efforts in finance and define areas of focus to help you achieve greater value. The process is covered in more detail in the book's conclusion.

Finance Leaders

- Is there a devoted position within your organization for a financial officer?
- Does your company have someone monitoring and recording financial documents and statements, such as a controller?
- Is your dedicated controller or financial executive a CPA?
- What qualifications do they have for the role?

The world of finance often gets a bad rap. I deal with finance because I like it and understand money. Still, many business owners look at their checkbook or do back-of-the-napkin-type accounting where they know how much money they have in their account and have a rough idea of expenses. The problem with that approach is that it's not a real, scalable strategy. One of my business-owner clients actually handed me a napkin when I asked to look at his financials. But you can't sell a napkin. There must be more than just the napkin.

People use software like QuickBooks or Sage 50 (formerly Peachtree) and begin keeping their debits and credits, which is a good start for your first week in business. But when we grow a company that we're going to sell, we have to go a little deeper. Suppose I wanted to sell a business that produced boiled peanuts (because I love boiled peanuts). In that case, chances are I'm not going to have the same accounting criteria that a publicly traded company like Whole Foods would have. They have to follow the Sarbanes-Oxley Act. I don't. Because Whole Foods follows the Sarbanes-Oxley Act's rigor, an investor may place greater confidence in the valuation's accuracy than my peanut company because I am not required to adhere to the same rigorous standard. As business owners, the closer you can align your accounting practices with the highest industry standard, the greater your potential value.

Finance Systems

- Have you developed and documented your company's financial plan?

- Does the financial plan help you to achieve the goals in your business plan? Is it aligned with your mission and values?
- What accounting systems are you using?
- Have you identified the actions necessary to accomplish the plan? How are your tactical plans aligned with the company's budget?
- Could the company raise additional capital?

I'm constantly tracking performance. I want to know where every dollar will come from and where that dollar will be deployed. Some years I'm well beneath my targets, while other years, I'm right in line with them. But I like to do it either way because it's part of a written finance strategy. I know where the dollars are going to flow, and I know of any potential obstacles. If you want to build a best-in-class business, you need to write out your company's finance strategy to show others what you're going to do with the dollars that are coming in.

We business owners are often not the accountant types. We're not big on crunching numbers. As a result, we need our financial systems to provide us with the information we need to make sound tactical decisions in our company. Your systems should minimize any barrier to actionable information so that you and your potential buyer can make sound business decisions.

Forecast and financial reviews

- Do independent audits or reviews take place at regular intervals?
- Are financial records prepared according to generally accepted accounting principles (GAAP)?
- Does your company have a system for annual financial forecasts? How often are these forecasts reviewed or updated?
- Do projections reflect economic reality?

GAAP is not an easy process and can cost money. We had a prospect who called us when they were ready to sell their business. They already had a letter of intent stating that their business would have to be prepared in accordance with GAAP accounting, but they were not. It was going to cost mid-six figures to make their business align with GAAP. If you're interested in driving your business's value, you should start preparing your financial statements in accordance with GAAP immediately. Of course, this could cost additional accounting fees, so incorporate this move as part of your strategic plan.

Financial Viability

- What is the company's gross margin? Is it flat or increasing?
- How profitable is the company? Has there been a trend, either upward or downward, on a year-by-year basis?
- How regularly are you creating cash flow projections?
- Has the company fallen behind on vendor payments? Other debts?
- Is your company on good terms with its lenders?
- How likely is it that the company will need to add new debt or equity financing in the next year?
- Does the company have enough cash accumulated to weather disruptions to the business?

Financial instability will reduce your company's value more than anything else. If you're trying to sell your company fast because you failed to anticipate an issue and you're bleeding money, you're not going to get a fair valuation. Financial stability involves the what-if scenarios, such as the COVID-19 pandemic that decimated the economy in 2020.[50] Did you have the cash to withstand the shock to your business? Most companies didn't, and they had to rely on the government to help them or else close.

Balance sheet

- Does the company have access to a capital line of credit? Is it enough?
- Are the days' sales outstanding usually greater than 45 days?
- Are trade payables usually greater than 60 days outstanding?
- Compared to your total capital, how much interest-bearing debt does the company have?

The balance sheet tells a picture of where you are today.

Internal management

- Are there documented internal protocols to prevent money from being lost or spent frivolously?
- Has the policy been updated in the last 12 months?
- Has it been reviewed and approved by the advisory board?
- Do you have a process that shows how dollars are going to be spent?

Give me a couple of days and I can usually find $15,000 to $20,000 in immediate savings in just about any business by using internal controls.

The Bottom Line

The financial side of your company covers a lot more than just money. Finance is also how sellable your knowledge and data, such as an email list, is. Finances tell a story about what you have dealt with in your business, where you're going, and ultimately what price your business will sell at. If you track only revenue, you can make all the money in the world but have no profit. You could show outstanding financial statements, but when the real story comes out, and it will, everything falls apart.

Action Item: Finance

Study your company's cash flow process—are you billing customers too quickly or slowly? Are your overhead expenses too high? Study your cash inflow and outflow and look for growth opportunities.

CHAPTER 9

Legal: Keeping Your Baby Safe

I f you operate your business as an entity (an LLC, a C corporation, a subchapter S corporation, etc.), you must abide by specific federal and state regulations. In fact, **the type of business entity you operate dictates the kinds of documents you must keep, the fees you must pay, and the taxes for which you are liable.**

If you are working to grow a best-in-class business, you must do everything possible to stay compliant with state and federal regulations. Doing so will protect your business entity and protect you in case of litigation. Showing a buyer that you have all the essential documentation that a prudent businessperson would have, especially if you're working with a reputable law firm, ensures that there won't be any significant skeletons in the closet if they end up buying the business. Having the legal systems of your business correctly structured increases the company's value and helps prepare, protect, and defend your business when life happens.

Here are **four steps** to make sure your business is compliant:

1. Hire a stellar attorney.

Hands down, the *best* way to protect your business is to hire a great business attorney. A sharp attorney will ensure your business complies with the laws that govern your particular jurisdiction. Additionally, they will make sure your governing documents are up to date and your agreements are correctly enforced.

2. Make sure your governing documents comply with state rules.

Thankfully, your attorney will help you create and enforce an operating agreement that tells people how the company should be operated and identifies members, shareholders, and officers. Additional areas of interest are often addressed in the operating agreement. These include different membership interest or stock classes, allocation of profits or losses, distributions, key management, rules for dissolution, buy/sale terms, restrictions on transfers, and so much more. It is vital to have your attorney review the documents regularly to ensure they remain compliant with state rules and regulations.

3. Make sure you've paid all required fees.

You need to make sure all your entity fees have been paid to the jurisdiction in which you are registered or domiciled. In Tennessee, for instance, business owners must pay an annual filing report fee based on their entity status. The report publicly records the ownership details of your company. If you fail to pay, your company could face state-mandated dissolution. If you are not sure what types of operating fees your company owes to the state or when the fees are due, check with your attorney or CPA.

4. Keep company and personal expenses separate.

I cannot say this enough—do *not*, I repeat, **do *not* commingle your personal expenses with your business expenses**. Your company is not your personal checking account. By keeping your personal and business income and expenses separate, you keep the "corporate veil" of protection in place. You've chosen to operate your company as an entity rather than as a sole proprietor, so keep your personal accounts separate.

If you choose to operate your business as an entity, do everything you can to protect the entity you've created. Rely on a stellar attorney to protect your interests. Prepare operating agreements and keep them compliant with state laws. Then, pay your state fees. And whatever else you do, do *not* commingle your personal and business expenses.

Employee Contracts: The Essential Elements

This one document could help you grow value above all others.

Many employers use employee agreements to protect their business interests and trade secrets, but more is at stake in these contracts. Sometimes called an employee agreement, an employment contract is a formal declaration that details the relationship between employer and employee. Typically, employers execute the arrangements for some time, such as one or five years, or make the agreement's lifespan indefinite.

Employee contracts have the advantage of controlling employee actions during their tenure with your company by clarifying their roles, responsibilities, and duties. You can also use employee agreements to enforce confidentiality, prevent high turnover, prevent competition, and protect intellectual property.

But you must remember that employee agreements legally bind business owners too. If you agree to specific bonuses, revenue sharing, or compensation plans, then you must be prepared to uphold your side of the bargain.

So, what exactly should you include in employee contracts? What provisions do you need to protect your business from potential harm? What do you need to clarify when employees begin to work for you?

18 Key Items I Recommend Including in Your Agreements with Your Employees

1. Type of employment (full- or part-time)
2. Term of employment (if applicable)
3. Business hours and number of work hours expected each week
4. Job title, duties, and responsibilities
5. Work product expected
6. The extent of service expected
7. Type of compensation (W-2, 1099)
8. Amount of compensation (hourly wages, salary, revenue sharing,

performance bonuses, etc.)

9. Benefits offered (medical insurance, life insurance, disability insurance, etc.)

10. Fringe benefits offered (time off, holidays, etc.)

11. Business expense reimbursements

12. Grounds for termination

13. Noncompete agreements

14. Nonsolicitation agreements

15. Nonacceptance agreements

16. Confidentiality agreements

17. Industry-specific regulatory agreements

18. Laws applicable to general employment or employment within a specific industry

Obviously, you should contact your business advisors and attorney as you implement employee agreements to make sure your interests are protected. Depending on your situation, you may need to add more provisions or include fewer provisions in your employment agreements.

How Do Employee Contracts Protect the Value of Your Business?

Just because you have employment contracts doesn't mean that employees will always abide by them, but they help protect you if a conflict arises that ends in litigation or mediation. Employee contracts also preserve the **value of your business**. The last thing a buyer wants to do is buy your baby only to have the babysitter, a key employee, walk out the door. Even more frightening is the babysitter walking out the door and asking the baby, your business, to follow.

Employment agreements assure the buyer that their investment is protected, but that doesn't mean you should wait until you are about to sell to have these agreements implemented! By delaying the implementation of formal contracts, your business value will be diminished. Just imagine that you have prepared your business for sale, only key employees refused to sign an employment agreement before the deal is consummated. I have witnessed this a few times. The business owner had to provide additional funds for that employee to get the business transaction completed, ultimately reducing the business's value.

Getting employee contracts signed on the front end helps ensure everything is above board and above reproach. It helps to establish an understanding between the employee and employer.

Business Contracts 101

Contracts exist everywhere! Every day, you enter into some type of contract. Whether you're making an online purchase or buying a hamburger, you essentially agree to a contract. When appropriately implemented, contracts can protect your secrets, reputation, property, equipment, and more.

Contracts don't just exist when you make a purchase or sell an item. They exist to **expedite**, **enforce**, and **ameliorate** any transaction between people. Here's what happens:

- First, there is an **offer** in every contract. Whether it's an offer to purchase or provide goods or services, hire or protect someone, or the like, there is an offer in every contract.
- Next, there must be an **acceptance of the offer** to make the contract binding.
- Then, there is a **consideration** of the offer. In other words, what are the terms and the conditions of the offer? Must the buyer pay immediately or within 30 days? Will the seller accept cash, credit, or check? Will the employees work five days a week or four days a week? Can vendors ship stock immediately or over some time?
- Within each contract, you will also have **mutuality of obligation,** or binding obligations, between parties. Maybe a buyer agrees to make payment for goods or services, or a seller agrees to provide goods or services. Perhaps employees agree to work so many hours a week or to keep company trade secrets to themselves.
- Beyond fulfilling obligations to each other, parties in a contract must possess **competency and capacity**. In other words, are both parties of legal age to enter into contracts, and do they have the

mental and financial capacity to abide by the agreements?

- Finally, for a contract to be fully enforceable in most circumstances, it must be **written**. My attorney always tells me, "If it's not written down, it didn't happen." If you want to protect your business interests, then have written contracts available to be signed by customers, vendors, suppliers, and the business owner. Don't be lazy. Just minutes of work writing out contracts can prevent years of legal headaches.

Why Contracts Matter to Business Owners

Each of the considerations listed above can create safety barriers around business owners. If you have all of your agreements documented, you can protect yourself from or during litigation. Furthermore, you can prevent customers, lenders, vendors, suppliers, and employees from taking advantage of you. The more protection you have around your business, the more valuable your business becomes. Essentially, by creating and enforcing contracts, you can build a best-in-class risk management department.

Debt and Value

As a small-business owner, you've probably dealt with financing as a borrower, and you may have even extended financing as a lender. Regardless of whether you're borrowing or lending, there are a few basics. More than likely, you've dealt with them either in business or in your personal life.

The key questions that need to be asked are:

- How much do you need to borrow?
- How are you going to pay it back?
- What are you using to secure the loan?

As business owners, we are often the creditor. If you provide service and don't collect cash either before the service or upon receipt and the customer doesn't pay you, you suddenly become a lender. You may have essentially given a 30- or 90-day interest-free loan.

Entrepreneurs looking to sell their business in the next five to 10 years often don't think about debt. Whenever you take on new debt or want to secure new debt, it will create some risk. You may assume that when you sell the business you're going to take the cash from the sale, pay off your debt, take the proceeds, and drive off into the sunset or that the buyer will assume your company's obligation.

That could happen in a perfect world. But what could muddy the water is something called a lack of assignment. Sometimes your debt cannot be assigned; you are personally attached to the debt and can't assign it to anybody outside of your name. Maybe you just purchased a new piece of equipment, and you got generous loan terms because you had excellent credit. You want to sell the company, and a qualified buyer offers you the full price, but now they can only get 60 percent financing. You choose to finance the extra 40 percent as a lender to the new buyer. Not only are you securing the business as a creditor, but you are still securing the latest piece of equipment, potentially personally, as an individual.

When I sold my first business, I sold all of the assets, including a Ford F-250. I didn't want to use my sales proceeds to pay off the truck, so the buyer and I had a special provision that said he would assume the truck's remaining liability. However, just because the business sales agreement stated he assumed liability, it didn't mean I was off the hook. In fact, I received a late payment notification about a year after the business was sold. Somehow the payment had not made it to the Ford company, and the company sent me the bill. Nothing nefarious was going on, but there I was, removed from the business for over a year, and I received a late payment notice. To make matters worse, the loan was still attached to my credit score, so I was not able to "assign" the liability. I've seen multimillion-dollar deals fall apart because of the assignability of debt.

To make matters worse, your planners, attorneys, CPAs, and CFPs will devise a plan to reduce your tax burden so that all the money you're getting from selling the company is not going to get eroded by the IRS. Because of all that planning, you may now be left holding a note on a piece of equipment you bought because of your excellent credit score but is currently unable to be fully paid off. I've seen this happen numerous times; you can't assume that just because a buyer's going to buy the business that they're going to pay off all your debt automatically. As a result, it could cause you to be in a position where you're not receiving top value for your company.

Debt affects the value of your business and is incorporated into the amount offered to the seller. There's something called enterprise value or company value that is used in the valuation process. This is the equation:

Enterprise value = market capitalization + market value of debt – cash and equivalents

Ultimately, debt is going to limit your selling options. Recently, I saw this happen to an individual in their 70s who had a reasonably large amount of debt. Two buyers stepped forward with interest in acquiring the business only to realize there was significant debt in play. Soon, both potential buyers began driving the purchase price down. Throughout the negotiations, the seller frequently said, "Oh my goodness, I just want to get out of debt." The seller couldn't walk away from the deal. They had to sell the business, and it ended up being a fire sale for the business owner.

When you're trying to close a business, the time between the offer and closing is your enemy. You want to get it done fast. Debt could delay you from realizing the value of your company you have worked so hard to grow.

Financing considerations in your business will affect the risk of your company, and risk affects value. Many people don't think of debt as risk management, but you should continually consider risk and its impact on value. Avoid exposure to risks as much as you can to help keep your baby safe.

How to Protect Your Business's Intellectual Property

If you own a business, you own intellectual property (IP) of some kind. At the very least, you have a copyrighted brand or a trademarked product. Perhaps you've invented the cure for cancer, or you've developed a secret formula for the world's best barbeque sauce. No matter what you've created, you need to take certain steps to protect your IP. The more proactive you are about securing your IP, the better chance you have of keeping it from your competitors.

I'm a huge fan of the show *Shark Tank*, which shows entrepreneurs pitching their business ideas to investors, or "sharks," like Mark Cuban, the Dallas Mavericks owner, or Kevin O'Leary, who cofounded the tech company SoftKey Software Products.[51]

On the show, people pitch their ideas to this panel of sharks, and the sharks will invest their money in the company they're interested in. Some of the ideas or products are awesome. Others don't hold up to questioning, and the sharks pass.

When an entrepreneur pitching to the sharks says they have some form of IP, the sharks almost always sit up and take notice, and not just because of liability protection. If someone is willing to jump through hoops to secure their IP, the sharks see commitment.

How to Avoid Lawsuits and What to Do If Your Business Is Sued

The word "lawsuit" can make even the mightiest business owners shrink to the fetal position in a dark corner. A lawsuit is one of a business owner's top-10 fears—up there with failure and change. These days, businesses are being sued more than ever.

Lawsuits alleging breach of contract, wrongful termination, discrimination, malpractice, harassment, misappropriation of funds, or any other reason can wreak havoc on your business. Lawsuits drain your company. They drain your time and legal expenses—even your positive energy. And, obviously, a lawsuit can cause a delay in selling. Many business owners considering selling their businesses can't sell if they're facing a lawsuit, because no one wants to buy a company that's in the middle of one. Some lawsuits could take a decade or longer to resolve.

That being said, let me walk you through ways you can mitigate your lawsuit risks.

Lawsuits vs. Litigation: What's the Difference?

Before I talk about how to mitigate your lawsuit risks, I want to clarify the difference between a lawsuit and litigation.

Technically, a **lawsuit** is a legal dispute between a plaintiff and a defendant that is brought to a civil (not criminal) court for judgment. Individuals, businesses, or groups of people file suit against a person, persons, or company they believe has wronged them. Once a lawsuit has been filed within a local, state, or federal court system, litigation begins.

Litigation is the process a lawsuit goes through once it's in the court system. It can involve securing legal counsel, gathering evidence, giving and hearing depositions, recording and reading affidavits, filing documents, procuring witnesses, and more. Litigation of lawsuits between individuals can last a couple of years or more, so imagine how lengthy litigation between individuals and businesses can last! When I was involved in a "business divorce" many years ago, litigation for my lawsuit lasted almost seven years!

Lawsuit and Litigation Costs

Discovery costs for small companies involved in lawsuits can cost **millions of dollars**.[52] I've seen several of my clients take customers to small-claims court for lack of payment. Typically, those clients spend between $3,000 to $15,000 on something deemed "simple." I've also seen small-business clients spend hundreds of thousands of dollars, year upon year, on litigation costs for lawsuits filed against them.

According to Business Practical Knowledge (BPK), "an average small business earning $1 million per year spends $20,000 on lawsuits each year."[53] BPK also mentions a study that the Klemm Analysis Group did that "estimates that perhaps as many as 52% of all civil lawsuits target small businesses each year." If those statistics don't catch your attention, I don't know what will!

How to Avoid Lawsuits against Your Business

Business owners are constantly at risk of being sued. You may not currently be worried about a lawsuit, but perhaps you should be. No matter how good a person you are or how upright your business practices are, you are not impervious to lawsuits. Anyone, at any time, for any reason, can file a suit against your company. I have seen lawsuits filed completely out of spite. So, when you are trying to maximize your business's value, one of the things you can do is try to avoid lawsuits. That's easier said than done.

Generally, I tell my clients to follow Patrick Fraioli Jr.'s advice in his article "Avoid Legal Time Bombs":[54]

- Have an experienced lawyer review your employment practices to expose any areas of weakness.
- Hire an intellectual property attorney to protect your IP and to help you avoid infringing on the IP of others.
- Have a lawyer review your business contracts, employee contracts, and employee handbooks for loopholes.
- Hire an attorney to help you develop a document retention policy for electronically stored information.
- Know how to look for fraud and how to implement internal controls to prevent fraud within your business.

Obviously, and perhaps most importantly, you need to have an attorney on your advisory team. Most likely you don't have a law degree, so you can't anticipate all your business risks. But a good lawyer can. A sharp attorney can help protect you and your business from lawsuits as much as humanly possible.

What to Do If You Are Sued

What happens if you are served? What should you do if someone files a lawsuit against you or your business?

- First, contact your attorney.
- After you consult with your attorney, you may need to file an insurance claim with the company that handles your business insurance.
- Then, keep your mouth shut. Don't share information about the lawsuit with people not involved in the claim. In other words, don't give the plaintiff extra fuel for his or her fire.
- Participate willingly in any investigation. Answer attorneys' and insurance representatives' questions adequately to provide the necessary information without giving unnecessary information.
- Finally, follow your lawyer's advice about what to do once liability is determined. Let your lawyer guide your actions regarding whether you will settle out of court or defend yourself in court.

Friends, I hope you never have to face litigation as a small-business owner. I can tell you from personal experience that being sued is a nightmare. Whether you are culpable or not doesn't matter. Any lawsuit you face can send you and your business into a tailspin. It's hard whenever people accuse you of wrongdoing. Business owners want to get the situation quickly resolved. Maybe you can get back on your feet; maybe you can't. Regardless of how protected you think you are from lawsuits, you should still "lawyer up." Have your attorney review your contracts, agreements, operations, and practices. Shore up your legal protections to protect both you and the value of your business.

Insurance Policies Small-Business Owners Don't Know They Need

Having the right insurance policies in place is all about protection. The more protected you are, the less CSR. Remember, less CSR equals greater business value. A prospective buyer is going to see whether you have the right plans in place. If you don't, they know they'll have to increase their insurance, which will create additional costs and reduce the company's revenue, which means that your business's value is going to fall. The buyers may also wonder what else you missed. If you didn't even get basic insurance—my goodness, child!—it's likely you're going to have other problems.

Here are the most common types of insurance:

- General liability: covers slips, falls, and other injuries suffered by customers and clients while on company property.
- Workers' compensation: insurance for employees who suffer job-related illnesses and injuries.
- Commercial auto: protection for business-owned vehicles.
- Property: coverage for multiple types of damage, including flooding, theft, and fire.
- Professional liability: protects professionals, like lawyers and physicians, against negligence and other claims.
- Cyber liability: covers against cyberattacks and data breaches.
- Employee practices liability: covers employers against claims alleging discrimination, wrongful termination, and other issues.

One or several of those insurances will most likely protect you and your assets if you are sued. They cover accidents, malpractice, theft, loss, and more. However, I propose that you need other insurance coverage types to mitigate the risks you could incur in business. Although different types of coverage may not cover you like general liability or a workman's comp plan would, they can be used to help protect some of your costs if lawsuits or business interruptions occur.

You need to work with an insurance agent to make sure you have the necessary policies, including the following insurance policies business owners don't always know they need.

Product liability

If you have a product-based business, then product liability insurance could help you. Essentially, this insurance covers lawsuits from customers who claim they have been injured by a product you produced, manufactured, or sold. Maybe you sell coffee, and it burned a customer's mouth. Perhaps you manufacture seat belts. What if a clipping mechanism in one of those seat belts malfunctioned in a car crash and led to a driver's death? Even if customers do not follow product directions or heed warning labels, they can still sue you if your product causes them injury. Therefore, I highly recommend asking your insurance agent if product liability insurance is right for your business.

Directors and officers (D&O) insurance

Most likely you are unfamiliar with this type of insurance. Simply put, directors and officer's insurance protects business executives from lawsuits resulting from their actions. Maybe an employee files a lawsuit against one of your executives for wrongful termination. Perhaps a different employee files a sexual harassment lawsuit against one of your business officers. Whether the lawsuits are justified or not, your business and its officers require the protection D&O insurance can provide.

Business owner's policy (BOP)

What if you don't work in a brick-and-mortar building? Instead, you operate a home-based business. In that case you wouldn't have a general liability policy or a property policy. You would purchase a BOP that covers your business property, general liability, and products. Taken as a whole, the BOP policy is one of the most popular and inclusive policies available for home-based businesses, and a good insurance agent can help you customize the BOP policy to meet your specific needs.

Home office policy

Similarly, if you operate your business from a home office and you have a little bit of traffic on site, you may want to purchase a home office policy. Not quite as inclusive as a BOP policy, the home office policy can cover some of your liabilities if accidents occur on your property. However, this policy does not cover natural disasters like a business owner's policy would.

Business pursuits endorsement

Also available to those with a home-based business is a business pursuits endorsement that goes on a homeowner's insurance policy. Probably the least protective of the home-based business insurances, the insurance rider may work best for a service-style business that doesn't have a lot of foot traffic or equipment.

Personal umbrella policy

If you secure no other policy as a home-based business owner, at least consider a personal umbrella policy. Typically sold in million-dollar increments, this policy places additional coverage limits over your home and your auto. Again, this policy won't protect your assets like other plans can, but it will help cover some costs in cases of accidents or lawsuits.

Business interruption insurance

Another insurance you may want to consider is business interruption insurance. Sometimes offered as a stand-alone policy and sometimes offered as an insurance rider to other policies, this type of insurance can provide you with financial coverage should natural disasters occur that interrupt your business operations. This insurance provides you with the income to help keep the company going and the employees paid. However, other insurance policies (like property insurance) will cover fixing or rebuilding any property attached to your business.

Flood insurance

If business owners protect themselves with business interruption, general liability, and property insurance, they think they have all of their interests protected. Flood insurance is coverage people don't think they need until they need it. Just remember, flood insurance covers you against water rising up from the ground, not from water raining down. For instance, let's say a tornado blows the roof off your building, and rain pours into your house. Homeowner's or business owner's policies would cover the rain flowing into your home or business. If the sewers backed up and water flooded from the street into your building, flood insurance would cover that. If rain causes the rivers to swell beyond their boundaries, then flood insurance is what you need, not BOP or homeowner's policies.

Life insurance

Once you leave the property and casualty insurance policies, you enter into personal insurance. In my opinion, every business owner should have a life insurance policy. As well as your own, you may also consider offering life insurance policies to key or all employees.

Business overhead expense (BOE) disability insurance

Additionally, I think disability insurance is vital for business owners. If employees depend upon you for their livelihoods and you get sick or injured, what happens to your employees? What happens to you? Not only will BOE disability insurance provide the business with income if you become unable to work, it will also provide income to keep employees paid or to bring in an associate to help keep the office operating.

Health insurance

Finally, you need health insurance. Whether you provide it to your employees is your decision, but at least procure it for yourself. It's a necessary evil, if you will. Even if you seem immune to illness, no one is immune to accidents or other people's negligence. Therefore, don't leave your health to chance. Don't let one hospital visit rob you of all of your business's profits. Take out health insurance on yourself to protect your business.

Conclusion

Although this list of policies is not exhaustive, I hope it helps you. You may need one or all of them. Contact your insurance agent, and make sure you have the right coverage in place. Don't leave your business assets unprotected. Protect your business from lawsuits, theft, accidents, disabilities, and risk.

How Legal Brings Value

The sample value-maximization process questions below can help you gauge your company's legal efforts and define areas of focus to help you achieve greater value. The process is covered in more detail in the book's conclusion.

Pending or past legal action

- Have any members of the company's leadership or its owners been convicted of a felony?
- Is the company facing unsettled legal action?
- Has the company been sued in the past? What was the outcome?

Your company's legal documents are a chance to protect your reputation, a form of risk management. Litigation, either pending or previous, could threaten your firm's viability and affect your company's value. Have you done everything to reduce your chance of litigation?

Intellectual property (IP)

- Are you tracking your intellectual property?
- Is it being legally protected? Have you created binding policies to ensure that intellectual properties created by employees belongs to your company?
- Is IP being actively used?
- Is research and development protected?

In my company, we have a lot of IP. We have books, courses, and many other things that we want to make sure are legally protected. You also have to protect what surrounds the IP, like research and development.

Contracts and agreements

- Have key employees signed noncompete and discretionary agreements?
- Have all contracts and agreements been reviewed by an expert?

- Are all employee procedures compliant with the law?
- Has upper management and managers been educated on their legal responsibilities?

Most people think about legal in terms of purchase and lease agreements, but legal is much more encompassing. Ensuring your company's contracts and agreements are up to date can protect you from costly or damaging information getting out or keep your employees continuing to work with you.

Filings, licenses, and disclosures

- Has the company's legal structure undergone review and approval by legal counsel?
- Is the company compliant with all regulatory bodies and jurisdictions where it operates?
- Have the company's licenses been maintained and kept up to date?
- Is the company in good standing with all income, payroll, and sales tax payments?
- Is the company responsible for regulatory filings? Have they been kept current?
- Are board meeting minutes adequately filed?

Your legal system is there to protect you from legal risk, whereas insurance is there to protect you from economic or systemic risk.

Risk Mitigation

- Does the company have a full business insurance package?
- Does the company use cloud storage for sensitive data?
- Is key data frequently backed up and tested for recoverability?
- Has a risk management review been conducted?
- Does the company have proper liability insurance?
- Are insurance policies reviewed annually?

The Bottom Line

To increase the value of your business, you must have the proper legal structures. Without the proper documentation with employees or the correct insurances in place, you could end up seeing everything undone with a simple, small loss. As such, solidifying and updating your legal structure leads to a direct increase in your company's value. Having proper contracts and knowing how to secure them could drastically increase the value of your company.

Action Item: Legal

Is your company meeting all compliance requirements? Be sure to double-check and maintain documentation. Having proper coverage and representation means being ready **just in case**. You never know what the future will hold, but it is essential to do anything and everything you can to reduce your company's—and your own—risk exposure.

HOW

CHAPTER 10

Strategic Planning: Making Your Baby Beautiful

S trategic planning is a process that creates the impetus of change by improving all **eight key areas**—maximizing the value of the company with all eight of your pizza slices. The previous eight chapters have prepared your mind for action. No doubt you have seen areas where you can work on your business. Without a framework or process, we business owners will quickly fall back into the poor business processes we seek to improve.

Enter Strategic Planning!

Strategic planning is a process used to identify the areas that can drastically increase a company's value. You may have questions about this process—it takes some time to understand it all—so I've included answers below.

So, Who's Involved?

Everybody in the organization at some point should be involved in strategic planning.

When Should Strategic Planning Happen?

I envision strategic planning as an annual event for my company, and I'll explain why. Every year, I meet with the team members in our organizations. We bring everybody together, allowing new individuals to see the vision— where we came from and what we're trying to accomplish.

More importantly, it allows me to share the one-year goal. Here's what we're trying to accomplish in the next fiscal year. Here are the revenue goals we're trying to meet. Here are the strategic initiatives we're trying to do. Here are the weaknesses or the threats we have to mitigate in the next fiscal year. Here are the problems I foresee.

We meet annually, and then we break those annual goals down to a quarterly level. This is not a concept I came up with all by myself; I read it years ago in *The Five Dysfunctions of a Team* by Patrick Lencioni.[55] Through the guidance of his book and my own experience, I've found that the best way for small-business owners to maximize their accomplishments is to meet annually, forecast what they want to accomplish, then revisit the objective quarterly. The team must frequently see what effects and changes they experienced from the last quarter.

How Important Is Preparing for Your Strategic-Planning Meeting?

There's a lot of homework to do before the meeting, in addition to the work that comes afterward. Preparation ahead of the forum will help get your team pointed in the same direction so there's no ambiguity. Someone once told me, "With no accountability, there is no responsibility," and that's exactly right. Once you've done this, everybody will know what they are required to do over the next year, and further, they'll know how accomplishing this goal will directly benefit them. But if you screw up this process by failing to prepare, your employees will view the strategic-planning meeting as a waste of time and be less motivated to follow through on your outlined goals.

Who Should Be Part of Your Company's Planning?

If you follow all the steps listed in the outline above, you'll have your hands full. You will need help, even if your company is small. Everybody in the organization should be involved in planning at some point. As a business owner, you want to determine your company's mission and vision based on your core values. Including your entire team and hearing insights from your managers and team members (or a business coach if you run the business alone) is vital to accomplishing your strategic-planning goals. By doing this, you can build a business where you are minimized, and your company's value increases.

But Why?

If you can get your whole team involved in the strategies, tactics, and actions that must be taken to accomplish your objectives, then you'll see more buy-in and commitment from them. If your team members understand your vision and mission, they can help you set objectives. Since they are the ones running the day-to-day operations of your business, they'll also be able to help you determine what actions are realistic to take. Proper strategic planning isn't a microwave dinner; it's a slow, methodical Crock-Pot recipe. In the end, it can yield higher-quality results.

When Should You Meet to Track Your Planning?

To ensure that strategic plans are communicated and reinforced, I suggest following a 1-4-12-52 model:

The 1: Annually

This is the meeting where you'll share your long-term vision, mission, and values with your team members. Often this is when you'll get them to buy in. Then, as a group, you can analyze your company's strengths, weaknesses, opportunities, and threats to set your three-year and one-year objectives, forecasting what you want to accomplish. Finally, you'll determine the short-term strategies, tactics, and actions needed to achieve your long-term goals.

The 4: Quarterly

Next, I like to meet with my team to follow up on my strategic-planning objectives quarterly. If you hold similar meetings, you can analyze how much you've accomplished over the past three months. Break your one-year goal into strategic quarterly pieces. Then, determine whether or not you accomplished what you set out to do within that time frame. Are your strategies working? Are you closer to achieving your goals? If not, revise your plan and set forth again.

The 12: Monthly

I like to meet with my team members yearly and quarterly; however, I also meet with them monthly. If you imitate my meetings, you'll break your goals into quarterly strategies and monthly action steps. In the monthly meetings, you'll hold your team members accountable, and they'll keep you accountable. Are you following the strategies that will help you meet your objectives? Do your actions fall in line with your vision, mission, and values? Are they getting you where you want to be? I find that team members feel empowered and that their morale goes up when they are encouraged to hold me accountable. High company morale leads to buy-in, which leads to a higher chance of reaching your company's objectives.

The 52: Weekly

Finally, I like to meet with my team weekly. If you hold weekly meetings, you can determine what each member must accomplish that week to meet your quarterly and yearly company goals. With these weekly meetings, you can keep everyone engaged and reminded of the long-term objectives.

Executing your strategic plans matters. By meeting yearly, quarterly, monthly, and weekly, you can keep your entire team on track to meet your long-term goals.

What Now?

If you're planning correctly, you can reinforce accountability across all avenues. Your team will feel empowered to hold you accountable, which is such a powerful thing. It's a morale booster for employees to see themselves as owning the mission together. There's buy-in, and no one is ever losing sight of the things the company needs to accomplish.

Everything has been broken down to a bite-sized scale. How do you eat an elephant? One bite at a time. That's what we're trying to accomplish here.

The Strategic-Planning Framework

There is a framework for the strategic-planning process we use in our company and in the companies we advise. It doesn't matter what type of business you own; the principles are universal. A practical and well-thought-out strategic plan should always go through this process. So, what are these vital steps to effective strategic planning?

For me, strategic planning can be broken into **eight key phases**:

1. Vision: Envision where your company will be in five years.
2. Mission: Write a mission statement.
3. Values: Write out your organization's values, and check them against your personal long-term vision and mission.
4. SWOT: Analyze the strengths, weaknesses, opportunities, and threats within your business.
5. Objectives: Pick three specific objectives you want to accomplish based on weaknesses revealed in your SWOT. I always make one of them financial.
6. Strategies: Brainstorm strategies that could achieve those objectives. Pick the top three.
7. Tactics: Write down three ways you plan to reach each of your objectives within a year.
8. Actions: Create three action steps you will take quarterly to help you accomplish each of your yearly goals. The process will help you reduce the business's enormous number of options to 27 measurable and accountable action steps, which are assigned to and received by the appropriate member of the team.

When you take the first letters of those phases, you've got an initialism I learned during my certified value growth advisor training: VMVSOSTA.[56]

Vision

If you're like me, you get ticked off when you hear so-called business consultants throwing the word "vision" around. In the past, they worked at a big company like General Electric when Jack Welch was there, and all of a sudden, they're like, "We always talked about vision when I was the VP of sales. Now let's talk about the vision in your small business."

I want to say, "Dude, you're wasting my time."

Forget all of that. Simply put, vision is your internal messaging of where you would like your business to be. Your vision could feel completely un-achievable, yet you, the owner, can see it. Maybe you would like to be the best-in-class technology company. Or maybe you want your business to influence legislative change. Whatever your long-term goal may be, write it down and communicate it with your team. I find that if I don't put my objectives in writing, they aren't getting done, a point that was hammered home in a Harvard MBA Business School study. The study showed that graduates with a set of written goals earned twice as much as their counter-parts who didn't have their goals in writing.[57]

Communicating your vision to your team is beneficial in many ways. For one, you will need their help to accomplish the vision. You may also find that involving your team in the strategic-planning process helps them buy in and increase team morale.

When I think about vision, I think about Charlie "Tremendous" Jones, a famed businessman and author whose seminars and books reached mil-lions of people during the mid- to late-twentieth century. Charlie was forceful, entertaining, and witty. He once said, "You will be the same per-son in five years as you are today except for the people you meet and the books you read." My mother took this statement and rephrased it for me. She would tell me, "Son, where you'll be five years from now is determined by the books you read and the people you associate with today."[58] Both Charlie and my mother realized that people could plan for the future; we can cast a broad idea for what we want to accomplish and make it happen. Since we're dealing with strategic planning, I'd like to modify Mr. Jones's words and my mother's saying: **where your company will be in five years is dramatically affected by the strategic planning you do today.** No matter how you say it, the message is vital.

Mission

If you don't already have a written mission statement, please take the time to write one. A mission statement is the messaging you want the public to know about your company. A solid mission statement should be realistic and achievable. You want people to believe that your company can accomplish its mission. It should be clear in its direction and lead to action. The people within your business should understand how to perform and interact with your consumers based on the mission statement. Finally, it should be motivating. Your team needs to feel that the mission of your company is worthwhile. The vision tells where you are going, but the mission statement is your *why*: your company's purpose. That's why it is so crucial in your strategic-planning process.

Walmart communicates its mission with the slogan "Everyday low prices." Nike wants you to "Just do it." Ford trucks are "Built Ford tough." My mind is often on pizza, and some pizza brands have memorable slogans. Pizza Hut: "No one out-pizzas the Hut." Domino's: "Get the door." Papa John's: "Better Ingredients, Better Pizza." (It's not better pizza, but it's still an effective tagline, in my opinion—prove me wrong.)

Missions are concise, memorable, and communicated publicly. They are a chance for everyone to know where they're headed.

Values

Many business owners mistake values for beliefs, but they're not the same thing.

Beliefs change with new information. At one time, most of the world believed that the earth was flat. As new evidence and data became available, our beliefs on that matter changed. However, values remain constant. You might value honesty and a strong work ethic. As a result, you are likely to work hard and carry yourself with integrity.

The values that you hold dear should be expressed through your business. As such, your vision and mission statements should align with your core values. I always recommend having a written values statement that you share with your team. Here are some of my company's values:

- *"Stewardship toward clients first."* We are client-centric, meaning our business's core is serving as a fiduciary to all of our clients. Being a fiduciary requires being bound ethically to act in the other's best interest. "Our influence is determined by how abundantly we place other people's interest first" (*The Go-Giver* Law of Influence).

- *"Grow the pie."* As we work as a team to grow the business, we all benefit from the team's success. We collaborate as a team through trust, honesty, respectfulness, love in communication, commitment to do our best in whatever we are tasked to do, accountability to one another, and acute attention to the team's results, helping where needed. "Our income is determined by how many people we serve and how well we serve them"[59] (*The Go-Giver* Law of Compensation).

- *"Turn the turtle."* When you come across a turtle that's stuck on its back, you turn it over. Likewise, when you see something that needs doing, you do it. Do not wait to be assigned. Do not expect that someone else will take care of it. Do not assume it is not in your job description. We value humility and work ethic.

- *"Leaders eat last."* As leaders, we will put the needs of our team above our own. "Your true worth is determined by how much more you give in value than you take in payment"[60] (*The Go-Giver* Law of Value).

- *"Don't touch the marshmallow."* When you choose not to eat the mini marshmallow in front of you for the sake of instant gratification, the reward ends up being larger for delayed gratification.

- *"Ability and attitude are greater than alphabet soup."* We take greater stock of a humble, hungry, skills, and "people-smart" attitude over the degrees and certifications beside someone's name. "The most valuable gift you have to offer is yourself"[61] (*The Go-Giver* Law of Authenticity).

- *"Teach others to fish."* Rather than being the sole resource that everyone depends on and would be devastated to be without, teach others how to gather for themselves. You provide value when you have an abundance mentality versus a scarcity mentality.
- *"Dive to the bottom."* Whenever there is a problem, don't just look for an easy fix. Dive to the bottom to understand the deeper issue and how it affects everyone and everything first.
- *"Find a way."* Be a "find a way, make a way" person. There is always a solution! There's got to be a way!
- *"Find a problem; find the solution."* If you see a challenge, don't bring it to others' attention until you also have determined a solution. Be solution oriented!
- "We will win." We have an abundance mentality! We can go further together than alone. "The key to effective giving is to stay open to receiving"[62] (*The Go-Giver* Law of Receptivity).
- *"There are only two things in life: results and excuses.... Excuses don't count."*

For example, Roy Disney, cofounder of the Walt Disney Company and Walt's older brother, is credited with a famous saying: "When your values are clear to you, making decisions becomes easier."[63] He wasn't talking about monetary value; he was talking about our interpersonal values—the things that drive us, the things that make us who we are.

Our personal values guide us along our journey. As we strive to become better, they help us visualize what we want in our future and ultimately how we're going to achieve it. Every person has values. Every one of us has an *ethos*, a core belief, a core being of who we are. Some of our values are good; some of them are not so good. Some of them are for the good of others, and some are for our good.

There are four types of values that drive us:

1. Individual

Our values provide us with specific individual needs. Yes, values can be self-serving, but that's not necessarily a bad thing. We all have unique needs. We need self-fulfillment. We have personal values that drive our humanity. They give us our passion and perseverance.

2. Relational

This type of value relates to relationships: how we treat the people close to us. Maybe it's openness. Maybe it's trust or kindness. Maybe it's honesty. I recently met someone whose every word was full of compassion. I was engrossed listening to them. His words revealed how much he cares for others.

3. Organizational

We also have work values. What are your priorities in the office? What motivates you to help your company succeed? Values help us develop our alliances and focus in the workplace.

4. Societal

Finally, we have societal values. We are aware of actions upon future generations. We pay attention to the environment and strive for sustainability. These are things we hold dear as a society. For example, I want my kids to understand what it's like to grow a garden because so many people don't have that opportunity, and my grandfather taught me that lesson. I think it's essential.

These four types of personal values—individual, relational, organizational, and societal—shape every aspect of your life. In fact, since our values affect our actions, they affect other people's lives too.

People exhibit positive values and negative values daily, but you have to be careful not to mistake beliefs for values. People frequently say, "I *believe* this is the case." However, that is an assumption based on their own life experiences. You see, beliefs are ever changing and based on information. New information comes in all the time, so you can change your beliefs based on that new information.

We seldom focus on values until we hear something negative, like investor Bernie Madoff ripping off thousands of people.[64] He was a crook, plain and simple. His values destroyed people's lives.

Values aren't always reflected in big things either. I know of people who, when they go to a hotel, steal all of the towels. My grandfather would say, "That's lack of character, son," but it ultimately boils down to values. I see more good than evil in the world. Maybe that's because I look for it. I love to see good, and I hate evil; I hate the lack of values it represents.

But we often see people do good things. We see companies that go way out of their way to be helpful.

There was an ice storm that hit northern Atlanta in 2014, stranding drivers. Cars were stuck there for hours and hours, and Chick-fil-A employees handed out sandwiches and biscuits to people who were stuck.[65]

We see people share these values daily, and they are so deep that they cut to your core. They're the things that define you, the code you live by, your ethos.

SWOT Analysis

As a business owner, you've probably heard of a SWOT analysis: a process where you identify your business's strengths, weaknesses, opportunities, and threats. But performing this analysis is nothing more than a time-consuming exercise unless you can put its results to good use. You need to spend time working to rectify those shortfalls.

I've gone through many SWOT analyses in my career. The coolest and the best way I've found to develop a SWOT analysis is to create a working process that gets your entire team involved. Allow them to ask challenging questions back and forth and don't take the first answer—make sure the question is being appropriately answered.

You may say, "Justin, I don't have a team. I'm by myself." You don't need to have employees to run a SWOT analysis. You can work with friends or family, as long as you have someone challenge your thinking.

A business and management consultant named Albert Humphrey is credited with introducing SWOT analysis at the Stanford Research Institute back in the 1960s and the 1970s using data from Fortune 500 companies,[66] so this technique has been tried and tested for 50-plus years. This is nothing new.

To construct an effective strategy to realize your long-term vision, you must understand your business's strengths, weaknesses, opportunities, and threats. During this step, it's imperative to view your business honestly and objectively. Now that you know the eight key areas of your business, I want you to assess your business's SWOT comprehensively. You want to capitalize on and protect your organization's strengths while improving its weaknesses. Likewise, you want to take advantage of opportunities while protecting yourself from threats to your business. The SWOT analysis is one of the most critical steps when creating your strategic plan because it provides you with definable targets to achieve your long-term vision. One of the hardest parts of a SWOT analysis is knowing where to start. Visit FinanciallySimple.com/swot/ to download a worksheet to conduct your own analysis.

The *S*—Strengths

The first step of the SWOT analysis deals with your company's strengths. What do you see as a strength of your business? What do you see as a strength from the point of the customer? What's a strength compared to competitors in the market?

When you're looking at strengths, you want to think about them in relation to your competitors, both internally and externally. You don't want to think about them in a vacuum. For example, if all your competitors provide a high-quality service or a high-quality product, then high-quality service or a high-quality product is not your strength. It's just the demand of the market. You've got to look at it in comparison with your competition.

What advantage does your company or organization have over your immediate competition? It may be size, volume, number of employees, the size of your sales, the quality of a product, or patents. There are several things that can be a strength. It's all about finding the quality that makes your business unique. There's a phrase I love, coined by television advertising pioneer Rosser Reeves, called the "unique selling proposition," or

USP.[67] It's what makes your company stand out and motivates a customer to switch to your company.

It can also be the location. I know one particular dentist whose office is located in a fantastic location—as soon as you come off the interstate, his office is right in front of you. That is an incredible competitive advantage. That is the strength of his company. Maybe you have different accreditations or certifications than the competition or have won national awards. As an Investopedia Top 100 financial advisor, I have a differentiation that other financial experts don't have in my marketplace. Likewise, I have been awarded The Exit Planning Institute's Leader of the Year Award.[68] How many financial or business experts can say that?

Once you get a competitive advantage, your competition will try to start chipping away at it, matching it, and maybe even surpassing it. Then you've got to find a new competitive advantage. If you're having trouble identifying your company's strengths, write down a list of your organization's characteristics and values. Then, write down your competitors' attributes and values. Compare the two. The items unique to your list will be your strengths—your competitive advantage.

The *W*—Weaknesses

Now let's deal with *W*, which stands for weaknesses, and those aren't always easy to tackle. I was watching *Winnie the Pooh* with my kids, and one of the characters found Eeyore's tail and tried to pin it back on him. The character said, "Oh, you lost your tail," and Eeyore says, "I probably didn't need it anyways."

If you're like Eeyore, you're able to see the weaknesses in everybody. If you're an eternal optimist, you don't count weaknesses the way you should. It's best to be realistic. You want to face the unpleasant truths now because your competition and customers can already see them.

Here are some questions that you may ask when you're trying to identify your weaknesses:

- What disadvantages do you have in comparison to your competition?

- Are they preying upon your weaknesses?
- Are they strengthening parts of their organization to fill in gaps your company is leaving in the marketplace?
- Do you have certain disadvantages?

Maybe you own a day spa, and your building is in a concealed location. Because of the obscure location, you must market more to draw customers to your place of business. Maybe that's the disadvantage, that you don't have a prominent location. But what *can* you improve on today?

You want to consider the weaknesses from an internal and external perspective. You want to look at your business through the eyes of your team, customers, and competitors. Imagine what your competitors are doing better than you.

By instituting a business-planning process within your company, you can disrupt today's weaknesses enough to make them tomorrow's strengths.

The O—Opportunities

After you deal with strengths and weaknesses, jump into opportunities: they're vital to your business's growth. A useful approach is to look at your strengths and ask yourself whether any of those strengths provide an opportunity for you to grow or become stronger. You can also look at your weaknesses and ask yourself, Do the weaknesses open up opportunities to eliminate the weakness?

You may wonder, What good opportunities can I spot? Maybe it's a growth initiative, a debt-reduction initiative, a team-building initiative, or perhaps a growth area has emerged because your competitor pulled back on its business. That might sound ruthless, but that's the way business works. It's a cutthroat environment. You want to keep an eye on the pulse and see if there are any ways that you can capitalize on other companies' misfortunes. Are there specific pain points in the niche market you're trying to reach? You may look at exciting trends, like technology. We have technologies today that in three seconds can do what used to take me a week.

Changes in government policy could present opportunities too. Sometimes they offer opportunities for business owners to consider moving their businesses to other states. Higher taxes in California are one reason why numerous companies, including Carl's Jr., have relocated to other states.[69]

I had a client years ago whose company had a military contract to make toothbrushes, but the government cut funding, and she lost the multimillion-dollar contract. We recognized that we had an opportunity to diversify the business to make toothbrushes for other vendors. They already had the programs, tools, and equipment. If the funding change hadn't happened, they might not have pursued those other opportunities. We entrepreneurs sometimes have blinders like racehorses do—all we see is what's right in front of us, and we miss chances to diversify our offerings. You saw that diversification amid the COVID-19 pandemic in 2020, when companies shifted to produce personal protective equipment and other supplies, doing everything they could to keep people safe and keep themselves afloat.[70]

The *T*—Threats

Threats are probably the hardest to forecast. Threats are external factors that come in and change or disrupt your business. The way I think of threats is to think of the word *pest*, like a mosquito. Consider those letters:

P stands for political.

E stands for economic.

S stands for social.

T stands for technological.

Regarding economic obstacles, are there quality or technological standards for your products that are changing? Is the economy undermining your business? One of the issues that I have to be constantly aware of in the financial world is that at any moment the markets could take a 20 to 40 percent dive, which could potentially cause revenues to drop significantly, such as the global financial crisis in 2020 due to the coronavirus pandemic.

The impact of the pandemic was difficult to forecast, and it caused many businesses to fail. They weren't prepared for revenue to evaporate. Other businesses planned ahead and could position themselves to survive the loss of business, or they were ready to pivot their operations and make the most of the situation.

Technology is fascinating because it can be an opportunity or threat, depending on the situation. My mother-in-law, for example, retired in part because of technology. She did not want to learn new nursing technology, and she said, point-blank, "I'm not going to learn these computer things. I've been a nurse for 40 years." The technology helps the hospital environment, but she didn't want to learn the computer processes, so she retired. That change was a professional threat to her.

A SWOT analysis won't capture every threat, but it can help you establish a plan if a threat does emerge. It is a chance to identify risk factors that could harm your company's revenue, profitability, growth, and value and to create plans to mitigate and manage those risks.

Objectives

As business owners, we have all fielded the question "What is your goal?" It's often difficult for people to answer. Sure, they have an idea about the direction they want to go; they have a vision, but seldom do they establish proper long-term objectives to bring those ideas and visions to fruition.

The takeaways from your SWOT analysis should be put to use when identifying the objectives you must reach on your way to your long-term vision. These objectives should be clearly defined and measurable because they will affect change for your organization's future. Many business owners choose to set their annual goals according to a theme. For example, you might focus on improving your sales processes and systems for one year and work to enter a new market the next.

Setting Long-Term Business Objectives

Designating objectives perhaps has the most significant impact on a business in that it helps you and your team members identify a central point of focus for the future. Setting objectives enables you to stay on your course. So how do you set objectives? More than that, how do you set achievable business objectives?

1. Think three years down the road.

It's been my experience that too many things can change within a time frame longer than three years. Sure, you'll experience ebbs and flows in your business over the course of three years, but not nearly as many as you will beyond that time. Therefore, set a business objective you know you can accomplish within three years.

2. Only set three goals.

Sticking with the number three, set only three goals when you're setting objectives. You may think that's a little crazy, but have you ever heard of the power of three? Think about it for a second. The number three is just about everywhere, and it's not accidental. Just look at the fairy tales you've heard since you were a child: "Goldilocks and the Three Bears," "The Three Little Pigs," and "Three Blind Mice." What about the three wise men of the Bible or the three musketeers? Why do teachers ask students to write three-point essays, or why do preachers preach three-point sermons? There's just something about the power of the number three. Maybe breaking ideas into three bite-sized pieces of information helps people commit that information to memory better. No matter the reason, the number three is powerful.

3. Make one of the three a financial objective.

When you're setting three objectives, make one of them financial so you can achieve quantifiable success. Maybe you want to increase your revenue by 3 percent or profit margins by 5 percent. The point is, by always including one financial goal, you will constantly be focused on your organization's bottom line while simultaneously working to increase its overall value.

4. Set objectives that align with your vision, mission, values, and SWOT analysis.

Make sure your objectives align with your vision, mission, values, and SWOT analysis. This is where all the work you've done in the strategic-planning framework comes into play. If you're setting objectives that counter your vision, you will never make it a reality. Likewise, if the objectives go against your organization's mission and values, your team won't be as likely to buy in, and your goals will be derailed. Last, if your objectives aren't addressing the weaknesses, opportunities, or threats to your business, then what's the point of setting them? You want your objectives to improve and strengthen your company in a way that drives you toward your vision and doesn't compromise your mission or values.

5. Have your management team set and create the objectives.

Another thing I recommend business owners do is to have their management team set the objectives. Unlike rank-and-file employees, owners and managers aren't worried about a handful of tasks. They're concerned about all tasks, divisions, and people. Your management team is trained and put in place to see the broadest views and the biggest pictures. They have the whole organization or division in mind rather than a snippet. Therefore, put them in charge of creating your company's objectives.

6. Apply the SMART filter to your objectives.

As you're setting your goals, follow SMART advice: make your objectives as *specific* as possible, create *measurable* objectives, make sure your objectives have *assignable* actions, create *realistic* objectives, and set a *time frame* for achieving your objectives.

7. Write down your objectives.

Finally, write everything down! As I said, if I don't put my goals in writing, I never accomplish them. And I'm not the only one. Dr. Gail Matthews, a psychology professor at the Dominican University of California, studied goal setting with 267 participants. She found that "more than 70% of the participants who sent weekly updates to a friend reported successful goal achievement (completely accomplished their goal or were more than halfway there), compared to 35% of those who kept their goals to themselves, without writing them down."[71]

Let me warn you: setting three growth objectives for your company is not an easy task. This portion of the strategic-planning process might take two days or more, and that's okay. Give yourself all the time you need because quality is more desirable than speed here. You're not running a race. You're setting goals for company growth. So brainstorm—write down any goals that come to mind. Most likely, you'll think of many reasonable goals, but not all the ideas you think about will follow the SMART filter, strengthen your weaknesses, or align with your mission and vision statements.

You want to set three goals that will direct and determine the future of your company. As you go through this process, follow these **five steps**:

1. Set goals that make your mission and vision statement a reality.
2. Set goals that strengthen your company's weaknesses.
3. Set goals that showcase your company's values.
4. Debate and filter through the goals you've written down. (This step will usually take longer than the first steps.)
5. Compile your final list of three objectives.

When you finish all five steps, you should have a working list of three company-wide objectives. This list is vital, but don't write down the objectives in stone. As you develop tactics and actions to accomplish your goals, you may realize one of the objectives is not measurable or realistic. When you assign employee tasks based on one of the objectives, you may recognize that the action step conflicts with your values. Don't worry; just rewrite, revise, or replace the objective that's causing you problems.

Reevaluate Your Objectives

Reevaluate the long-term goals and action items you've established. You may be able to use them in developing your objectives for the future. Do the objectives follow the structure outlined above? Are they SMART? Measurable? Are one or more of them financially focused? Do they align with your vision, mission, values, and SWOT analysis? It will take some time to settle on and finalize your key objectives, but a good starting point is the business areas that you'd wish to improve.

Start Working on Your Business

Jeff Bezos, founder and executive officer of Amazon, once said, "What we need to do is always lean into the future; when the world changes around you and when it changes against you—what used to be a tail wind is now a headwind—you have to lean into that and figure out what to do because complaining isn't a strategy."[72] I fully agree—I could almost feel a mic drop right there. That statement is powerful by itself. We often fuss about things in our way instead of trying to figure them out. Complaining is *not* a strategy. Strategies are plans of action. It's time to stop complaining about your business and start working on your business by developing strategies to grow your business.

At this stage, you and your team should have a clear vision that is supported by your mission and values. You should understand your strengths, weaknesses, opportunities, threats, and what needs to be done to improve them. Now you need to have a brainstorming session with your team to find strategies to meet your newly determined objectives. Selecting the right strategy will help you reach your goals by providing you with a road map of getting to your destination.

We want to achieve our three objectives, so we're going to start strategizing. *How* are we going to achieve those goals? I want you to answer three questions:

1. How will we engage with our customers?

Your methods could include operational excellence, product leadership, and customer intimacy. This strategy is called the value disciplines model:[73]

Operational growth

Companies with operational excellence are reliable, and their logistics are dominant. With McDonald's, you can consistently get the same hamburger across the world. Walmart is consistent; you know pretty much what they have to offer.[74] These companies have streamlined their processes and have the lowest cost structures among their competitors. They have the lowest prices. They have supply chain management.

They deal with large volumes. They're speedy; they're reliable. They can duplicate the process over and over and over again.

Product leadership

You can also engage clients through product leadership, which involves research and development—think Apple or Tesla. At this point, Tesla is an expensive vehicle. Apple watches can be costly too! I thought about buying one, but looking at how much they cost wore me out. These brands have flexibility in production and product innovation and typically have the best product. A product-innovative company is one that's focused on innovation. Investing in state-of-the-art products and services requires high investments in your research and development arms. You're dealing with performance and leadership. You often market your brand. Does this sound like an Apple or a Samsung?

Often, you're dealing with high margins in a short time frame because your competitors very quickly copy the product. You'll see a cooler called the Yeti in many outdoor sporting stores in the hunting and fishing world. Yeti produces an exceptional product. Their research and development are outstanding. I got a knockoff Yeti because I wasn't going to pay $600 for a cooler. I purchased two coolers for $200 at a Christmas sale from a new company that copied what Yeti was doing but modified the product slightly. Yeti wants to be the top product, and if they don't continue to do research, development, and innovation, the company will fall from its industry pinnacle. It's the same with Apple; there are too many other companies nipping at their heels.

Customer intimacy

You have a deep understanding of your customer's needs, and you developed customized products for them specifically. Instead of striving to be the lower-cost leader, you are dealing with above-average pricing. If I purchase an Apple device, do you think Apple gives a flying flip about Justin Goodbread? Probably not, but if I go down the road to a local hometown diner on a Friday night when they're serving frog legs, the waitress will recognize that I'm that financial guy who lives down the road. Or if I go to the nearby co-op and get some chicken feed or some hay for our critters, "the Preacher," as I call him, behind the co-op counter will say, "Son, where's your family? Where are those cute little kids? You must have the boys working," and we'll laugh and shoot the bull. That's customer intimacy: a personal connection—and, as the consumer, I pay a little more for the relationship.

A Difficult Choice

How are you going to engage with your customers? As you move up the paradigm, you're looking to become a trusted business through your strategic planning. Are you going to be customer-centric? Are you going to be a low-price leader? Are you going to be focused on research and development? There's nothing wrong with any of these options; it's merely a personal choice.

2. How will we be positioned in the market?

As you bring your objectives to life and try to create a strategy to move this forward, how will you be positioned in the market?

There's a strategy called the Bowman's clock strategy or Bowman's strategic clock that is often used in marketing to analyze a company's competitive position in comparison to the various offerings that the competition may use. It was first highlighted in a 1997 paper by Cliff Bowman and David Faulkner. This "clock" has eight different positions instead of 12, and each of the positions corresponds with a quality reflecting high or low perceived value to the consumer.[75]

Instead of 12 at the top of the clock, it starts with one in the lower-left corner, representing something with low price and low added value, like a dollar store. As we travel clockwise to two, the perceived value to the customer starts increasing. By number three, the price is beginning to increase slightly, and the customer is beginning to perceive more value. If Walmart is a two as a low-price leader, a hybrid store will have more perceived value, although the price is just slightly more expensive: think Target. The quality of goods at Target is thus perceived to have a little more value.

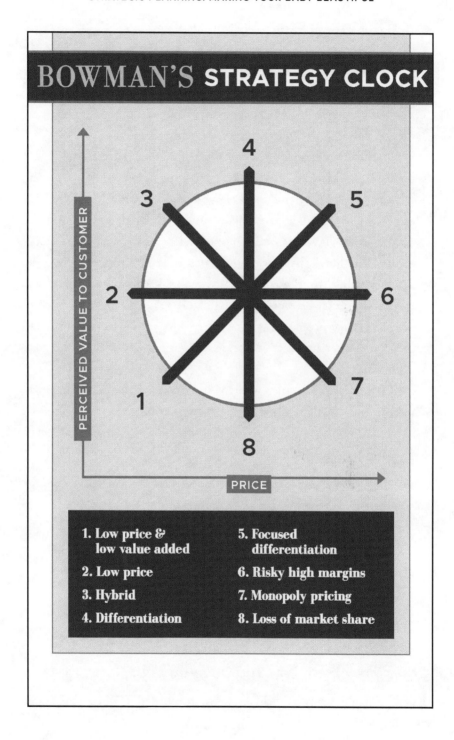

3. How are you going to grow?

"Growth" isn't referring to monetary growth here. Sometimes you have to grow your company by developing new products or entering new markets. If you recall from the earlier illustration, the tape maker 3M was originally a mining company. However, over 100-plus years they've had to restructure their company multiple times.

On the other hand, there's Blockbuster. I remember it was a big deal to go to the Blockbuster store and get a movie when I was growing up. You would take home the VHS and put it in the tape player. Then came DVDs, then companies like Netflix, which changed the model for movie rentals. Then streaming came along and changed the model further. Wouldn't it have been something if Blockbuster, all those years ago, had said, "You know what? Instead of keeping these big stores, we're going to create a new product. We're going to create these crazy little boxes that people can walk up to at Kroger or Walmart, put some money in, and rent movies curbside. Or rent movies through the mail. Or livestream."

If Blockbuster had tried to pivot and make a new product in a new market, they might be in existence today. They didn't, and they're gone.

Risk and Reward

According to a strategic-planning tool called the Ansoff matrix, to engage customers and achieve market penetration, future growth opportunities can emerge in four ways:[76]

1. The same products/services to the same markets
2. New products/services to the same markets
3. The same products/services to new markets
4. New products/services to new markets

Other Models to Help You Develop Your Strategies

There are many, many models to choose from. A few others you might consider include the following:

- Balanced Scorecard: this framework accounts for your objectives, measures, and initiatives. You can then track your results, as well as the consequences that crop up as a result.[77]
- Strategy Map: a visual way to outline strategies and goals that is easy for everyone to follow. The top grouping deals with financial goals, followed by customer desires, internal strengths, and learning and growth needs.[78]

What Next?

By deciding *how* you will engage your customers, position yourself in the market, and grow your company, you will develop strategies to meet your business objectives. Remember, complaints don't solve problems; strategies do. Once you know *how* you're going to meet a goal, you can decide *what* you will do and *who* needs to do it.

Tactics

With your objectives defined and a few strategies selected to guide your team to success, it's time to choose three tactics that will drive you toward your three-year objectives. Tactics are the tangible directives of your strategies.

Your company's tactics and actions cannot be developed by the person in the corner office. I call it the ivory tower effect when managers sit in their corner office, away from their employees. Instead, the *how* of a tactic must be developed by those actually doing the job.

Once you and your management team have set goals and developed long-term plans to meet those goals, it's time to bring in your team members—the ones doing the company's day-to-day work. Now is the time to share your business objectives and get feedback. You're not asking your team members whether or not they agree with your goals. Obviously, you want them to buy into your holistic objectives; it's imperative if they work with you. In this instance, though, you want them to help you determine ways to accomplish your goals. Another way I could illustrate this concept

IVORY TOWER EFFECT

is as follows. The business owner is defining the "what" and "why" of the business, yet the owner is seeking the expertise of the team to help determine the "how."

Your team members are in the trenches of your business, so they know the processes and procedures that keep your company running like a well-oiled machine. If they understand your goals, they can show you how to reach them. Furthermore, your team members will know who should work on each task and actionable step. They're the best ones to help you create tactics and actions.

Stepping into Action

Once you have identified the three tactics for each objective, you will choose three action steps for each tactic. Choose three action steps that will take you through the next quarter. Your action steps should be achievable within a 90-day time frame, and they should be directed toward accomplishing your tactics, which are directed at achieving your objectives, which are driving toward your long-term vision. As you can see, there is a lot of meticulous work involved in strategic planning, and each step in the framework works to achieve the desired outcome of the previous step.

Let's assume that one of your business objectives is to increase your company's profit margins by 20 percent. (Remember, one objective must be financial!) How will you do that? What's your *strategy*? Well, **to increase your company's profit margins, you're going to have to increase sales and decrease expenses**.

Managers that are too far from the problem will find it difficult to build effective solutions.

Objective 1: Increase gross profit margins by 20 percent.

Tactic 1: Increase brand awareness.

First action: Social media team to incorporate company logos in all posts by end of the first month of the quarter.

Second action: Marketing team to create new product packaging with the company logo within 60 days of this meeting.

Third action: Floor team to repackage products with newly branded materials by quarter's end.

Tactic 2: Decrease expenses by 5 percent.

First action: Finance department to audit corporate expenses to find and eliminate frivolous spending, proving detailed reports by the end of the second month in the quarter.

Second action: Owners to review insurance options and pricing with an agent by the end of the second month in the quarter.

Third action: Business manager to renegotiate vendor costs and contracts within 30 days of this assignment.

Tactic 3: Increase sales by 5 percent.

First action: Marketing team to create an advertising campaign to show off slow-moving products within 15 days.

Second action: Sales team to bundle related products into sellable packages and work with marketing to improve the efficiency of sales by 12 percent within 60 days of this meeting.

Third action: Owners to add a commission incentive for salespeople who sell $X in a week's time frame and verify the new commission schedule's impact with the finance department for a quarter-end rollout.

Tactics and Actions Matter

Your tactics will remain throughout the year, but your action steps can be accomplished more quickly than that. You can accomplish some of your action steps within a week, a month, or a quarter's time frame. Therefore, once you cross an action off your to-do list, create a new action step to take its place.

Unless you create super specific, measurable steps to follow, you'll take no steps forward, and you have to move forward if you're working to increase the value of your business. Strategic planning helps you clarify your vision and mission, identify your current state of affairs, clarify your objectives, and take action steps to achieve them. It helps you move forward and grow the value of your company.

Value-Maximization Process (VMP)

Now that you understand the aspects that make a company like yours more attractive to prospective buyers—as well as how to improve the areas where your business is less attractive—it's time to put that knowledge into action. However, even with this understanding, it can be incredibly difficult to set aside your biases when working on something you're so emotionally connected to.

This is why our company uses a VMP to help remove the personal biases and emotions (something we all struggle with when someone is talking about our baby) out of the equation and to focus on quantifying a company's risk and value. That process centers on **six steps**.

Step 1. Comprehensive X-Ray

The comprehensive X-ray goes through all eight major areas that we've identified and takes 54 to 250 data points into account that we can use to assess a business. Typically, the assessment will take several hours. It allows the business owner to look at their business the way an investor, banker, or potential partner will. It's an in-depth view of how the company operates.

Step 2. Quantification of assessment

The second thing we must do is quantify the information the assessment yields. At this point, we start scoring each of the eight areas to determine where we need to focus our immediate attention. It's not uncommon as we go through the assessment to uncover problematic areas that the business owner never dreamed of, and we have to tackle those first. I call that the low-hanging fruit. You may want to go in and deal with the low-hanging fruit first so you can get onto big wins, or you may want to take on something more strategic.

Step 3. Prioritization of improvements

The assessment results allow prioritization of action. We typically recommend listing items of attack from zero to 10 or zero to 20, depending on the company's size. This is still only involving the business owner or the management team at this point.

Step 4. Strategic planning

After we identify what we're going to attack, we will bring the company together for strategic planning. The strategic plan could involve the entire team or individual departments at a time. The strategic-planning process will provide us with the order of correction that we need to adopt to help move the company forward.

Step 5. Motivation

The strategic-planning process will yield 27 tactics per department or per company. It then becomes a matter of motivation. Trust me; business owners must be consistently motivated not to fall back into the old routine of action. Remember, we've accepted the statement "To affect the future, you must disrupt the present," and so that's what we must continue to do here.

Step 6. Repeat

This a repetitive process! The repetition could take place on an annual basis. Many small businesses can only handle about one of these processes per year. Still, if you're in a company with multiple departments that have well-established department heads, maybe you could go through the process two or three times a year.

Road Map

The VMP includes recommendations for all eight categories and all the subcategories. It is a road map that will help you drive up the value. These eight categories, when working in tandem, can help you drive and uncover strategic value. At the same time, the sum of the whole is greater than the individual parts.

As you work through your short-term and long-term improvements, you can focus on making your company profitable, sustainable, and scalable as you prepare to sell your business for maximum profit.

By the end of the strategic-planning process, you should have a written document that, if implemented, will drastically change the direction of your company.

Conclusion

Your baby is all grown up. Congratulations!
This wasn't an easy process. Take a moment. Pat yourself on the back. Think about how far you've come. Remember: this strategic plan is a working document! Make sure you revisit your plan at least every 90 days. Going through the strategic-planning process will help you rise above the pack—it puts you in a position to beat the odds when you decide to sell your company.

Follow the steps and put in the work, and you'll be able to demonstrate previous growth and a path forward, which becomes a proven, documented road map of your business's past success. You'll substantially increase the odds that your "retirement ticket" is worth buying.

I want to hear about your company's progress. If you have any questions or feel like you could benefit from one-on-one coaching, feel free to reach out to me at JustinGoodbread.com.

Value-Maximization Results—An Owner's Narrative

Jerome was like a lot of business owners; he got caught being the fireman, putting out every fire. He was tired. He'd gotten to the point where, as Michael E. Gerber famously wrote in his book *The E-Myth*, "If your business depends on you, you don't own a business—you have a job. And it's the worst job in the world because you're working for a lunatic!"[79]

Jerome felt that way. It seemed to him like there was no hope, and he needed help. Plus, he was broke. All of his money went into his business. So, over six years, we restructured so he didn't have to operate within the company. He reached a point where he could sell his business, but **he**

didn't want to because he found joy in operating it once again. He had a company that could function without him present. He loved it.

Time passed, and he was finally doing the things that he initially set out to do. He previously didn't have freedom—he now made all eight areas of his business stand-alone silos running at maximum efficiency. He had documented everything and did everything by the book. His revenues grew. Profitability grew. His time grew. His team's efficiency grew. His joy grew. Everything grew in the right direction.

After enduring the hard work, after pushing the boulder up the hill, the day came when somebody approached him and said, "We've been watching your business. We'd love to buy it." He smiled. "It's not for sale." Six years before that he would have given it away. But the gentleman drove a hard bargain, and Jerome entertained the offer. When they reached the negotiating table, the business appraised for four times what it had six years earlier.

Jerome sold his business after accomplishing his goals and ambitions. He went on to start another business. Only, this time, by employing the principles outlined in this book from the onset, the company skyrocketed.

By focusing on value maximization, Jerome learned an important truth: value maximization is just good business.

Endnotes

1   Scouler, Dan. "The Frequently Fatal Family Business Flaw: Denial." Entrepreneur, February 25, 2014. https://www.entrepreneur.com/article/231757.

2   Biery, Mary Ellen. "Study Shows Why Many Business Owners Can't Sell When They Want To." Forbes, February 6, 2015. https://www.forbes.com/sites/sageworks/2017/02/05/these-8-stats-show-why-many-business-owners-cant-sell-when-they-want-to/.

3   BizBuySell. "Small Business Study: 2018 Small Business Owner & Buyer Demographics." May 31, 2018. https://www.bizbuysell.com/2018-Small-Business-Owner-Buyer-Demographics.s

4   Snider, Christopher M. "Walking to Destiny: 11 Actions an Owner Must Take to Rapidly Grow Value & Unlock Wealth." Exit Planning Institute, 2016.   https://www.exit-planning-institute.org/wp-content/uploads/2017/01/Walking-to-Destiny_Chapter-1.pdf.

5   Key Private Bank. "Do You Have Realistic Expectations about Your Company's Value?" 2016. https://www.key.com/kco/images/Business_Value_Optimization.pdf.

6   Guidant Financial. "Boomers in Business – 2020 Trends." Accessed December 28, 2020. https://www.guidantfinancial.com/small-business-trends/baby-boomer-business-trends/.

7   Toland, Bill. "Baby Boomers Creating 'Silver Tsunami' in Workforce." Pittsburgh Post-Gazette, December 21, 2014. https://www.post-gazette.com/business/career-workplace/2014/12/21/Baby-boomers-creating-Silver-Tsunami-in-workforce/stories/201412210003.

8   Internal Revenue Service (IRS). "Valuation of Non-controlling Interests in Business Entities Electing to Be Treated as S Corporations for Federal Tax Purposes." Accessed December 29, 2020. https://www.pvfllc.com/files/IRS_Revenue_Ruling_59-60.pdf.

9   Berkshire Hathaway. "Berkshire's Corporation Performance vs. the S&P 500." February 27, 2009. https://www.berkshirehathaway.com/letters/2008ltr.

pdf.

10   Pratt, Shannon P. *Valuing a Business: The Analysis and Appraisal of Closely Held Companies*. New York: McGraw-Hill Education, 2007.

11   Hicken, Melanie. "Workers Spend More Time Planning Vacation than Retirement." CNN Money. August 19, 2014. https://money.cnn.com/2014/08/19/retirement/401k-investments/index.html.

12   Carufel, Richard. "Time Management: A New Survey Reveals How Biz Owners Are Spending Their Time—And How They'd Rather Spend It." Agility PR Solutions. February 26, 2016. https://www.agilitypr.com/pr-news/business/time-management-new-survey-reveals-biz-owners-spending-time-theyd-rather-spend/.

13   Exit Planning Institute. "The State of Owner Readiness." 2018. https://www.exit-planning-institute.org/state-of-owner-readiness/.S

14   Nixon, Richard. *Six Crises*. New York: Touchstone Books, 1981.

15   Hunt, Brian. "Revisiting the Iceberg of Ignorance: Has It Melted Yet?" LinkedIn. September 29, 2015. https://www.linkedin.com/pulse/revisiting-iceberg-ignorance-has-melted-yet-brian/.

16   Kirby, Jason. "CEOs: Stop Quoting Wayne Gretzky's 'Where the Puck Is Going' Quote." Canadian Business, October 3, 2014. https://www.canadianbusiness.com/blogs-and-comment/stop-using-gretzky-where-the-puck-is-quote/.

17   Miller, Jo. "Leaderly Quote: If Your Actions Create a Legacy ..." Be Leaderly. 2019. https://www.beleaderly.com/leaderly-quote-actions-create-legacy/.

18   Seamon, Terrence. "Leaders, Honor Thy People." About Leaders. January 28, 2016. https://www.aboutleaders.com/leaders-honor-thy-people/#gs.qa-ca0m.

19   YouTube. "Be All You Can Be." April 14, 2016. https://www.youtube.com/watch?v=ms9pxvEbILs.

20   Rainer, Thom S. "Fourteen Indispensable Leadership Quotes from Jim Collins." Church Answers. December 3, 2012. https://www.churchanswers.com/blog/fourteen-indispensible-leadership-quotes-from-jim-collins/.

21   Collins, Jim. "Good to Great: Fast Company." Jim Collins. October 2001. www.jimcollins.com/article_topics/articles/good-to-great.html.

22   Fleming, Anthony. "Are You an Effective Leader?" Anthony Fleming.

2020. https://www.anthony-fleming.com/are-you-an-effective-leader/.

23   Thorpe, Doug. "Great Leaders Don't Set Out to Be a Leader." Doug Thorpe. September 17, 2019. https://www.dougthorpe.com/great-leaders-dont-set-out-to-be-a-leader/.

24   Meier, JD. "Management Is Doing Things Right, Leadership Is Doing the Right Things." Sources of Insight. 2020. https://www.sourcesofinsight.com/management-is-doing-things-right-leadership-is-doing-the-right-things/.

25   Scouler, Dan. "The Frequently Fatal Family Business Flaw: Denial." Entrepreneur.com. February 25,2014. https://www.entrepreneur.com/article/231757

26   Collins, Jim. Built to Last: Successful Habits of Visionary Companies. New York: Harper Business, 1994.

27   Google/CEB. "The Digital Evolution in B2B Marketing." Think with Google. October 2012. https://www.thinkwithgoogle.com/future-of-marketing/digital-transformation/the-digital-evolution-in-b2b-marketing/.

28   "It's Your Attitude, Not Your Aptitude, That Determines Your Altitude - Courting Business." O'Reilly. 2020. www.oreilly.com/library/view/courting-business/9781564147991/xhtml/ch04.html.

29   Goodbread, Justin. "Changing to a Modern Sales Process from a Traditional Sales Process." Financially Simple. January 24, 2019. https://www.financiallysimple.com/traditional-sales-process-to-modern-sales-process/.

30   "Marketing." Lexico by Oxford English Dictionary. accessed September 9, 2021. https://www.lexico.com/en/definition/marketing.

31   Twin, Alexandra and Somer Anderson, eds. "The 4 Ps Definition." Investopedia. July 7, 2020. www.investopedia.com/terms/f/four-ps.asp.

32   "Marketing Theories – The Marketing Mix – From 4 Ps to 7 Ps." Professional Academy. accessed September 9, 2021. https://www.professionalacademy.com/blogs/marketing-theories-the-marketing-mix-from-4-ps-to-7-ps/.

33   Google/CEB. "The Digital Evolution in B2B Marketing." Think with Google. October 2012. https://www.thinkwithgoogle.com/future-of-marketing/digital-transformation/the-digital-evolution-in-b2b-marketing/

34   IHOP. "IHOP Changes Name to IHOB and Reveals the 'B' Is for Burgers." June 11, 2018. www.ihop.com/en/news/2018/ihop-changes-name-to-ihob-

and-reveals-the-b-is-for-burgers.

35   Rico, Will. "How Much Should Small Businesses Spend on Marketing?" CommonMind. December 3, 2020. www.commonmind.com/blog/strategy/small-business-marketing-budget/.

36   Russo, Ralph D. "Walk-Off: Alabama Beats Georgia in OT for National Title." ESPN. January 9, 2018. www.espn.com/college-football/recap?gameId=400953415.

37   Maxwell, John C. The 21 Indispensable Qualities of a Leader: Becoming the Person Others Will Want to Follow. Nashville: Thomas Nelson Inc., 2007.

38   Adams, Kirk. "Helen Keller: 'Alone We Can Do So Little. Together We Can Do So Much.'" AFB Blog. American Federation for the Blind. June 26, 2018. www.afb.org/blog/entry/happy-birthday-helen.

39   Goldberg, Joel. "It Takes a Village to Determine the Origins of An African Proverb." Goats and Soda (blog). NPR. July 30, 2016. www.npr.org/sections/goatsandsoda/2016/07/30/487925796/it-takes-a-village-to-determine-the-origins-of-an-african-proverb.

40   Goodbread, Justin. "Understanding Positive Company Culture - Rising Above Dysfunction." Financially Simple. February 18, 2019. www.financiallysimple.com/understanding-positive-company-culture/.

41   Doyle, Alison. "Company Culture: What Is It?" The Balance Careers. September 17, 2020. www.thebalancecareers.com/what-is-company-culture-2062000.

42   Andersen, Erika. Growing Great Employees: Turning Ordinary People into Extraordinary Performers. New York: Portfolio, 2007.

43   Marriott. "J. Willard Marriott." Accessed September 9, 2021. www.marriott.com/culture-and-values/j-willard-marriott.mi.

44   Samuels, Doug. "Nick Saban Breaks Down What 'The Process' Really Is, and Where His Belief in It Began." Football Scoop. January 31, 2018. www.footballscoop.com/news/nick-saban-breaks-process-really-belief-began/.

45   Matthew 6:21 (NIV).

46   Drury, Amy. "Operations Management Definition." Investopedia. September 6, 2020. www.investopedia.com/terms/o/operations-management.asp.

47   Tennessee Wildlife Resources Agency. "Trout Fishing in Tennessee." Jan-

uary 13, 2021. www.tn.gov/twra/fishing/trout-information-stockings.html.

48   Sanginario, Ken. Certified Value Growth Advisor (CVGA) handbook. 2018

49   "The Four Faces of the CFO." Wall Street Journal, October 20, 2011. www.deloitte.wsj.com/cfo/2011/10/20/the-four-faces-of-the-cfo/.

50   Winck, Ben, and Juliana Kaplan. "How COVID-19 Decimated the US Job Market: Long-Term Scars and Effects." Business Insider. December 31, 2020. www.businessinsider.com/economic-outlook-labor-market-permanent-dam-age-coronavirus-unemployment-recession-recovery-2020-12.

51   ABC. "Watch Shark Tank TV Show." Accessed September 9, 2021. www.abc.com/shows/shark-tank.

52   US Courts. "Litigation Cost Survey of Major Companies." Duke Law School. May 10, 2011. www.uscourts.gov/sites/default/files/litigation_cost_survey_of_major_companies_0.pdf.

53   Practical Business Knowledge. "Lawsuits in Small Business." 2020. www.businesspracticalknowledge.wordpress.com/legal-security/lawsuits-in-small-business/.

54   Fraioli, Patrick A. "Avoid Legal Time Bombs." Entrepreneur, November 6, 2008. www.entrepreneur.com/article/198352.

55   Lencioni, Patrick. The Five Dysfunctions of a Team: A Leadership Parable. San Francisco: Jossey-Bass, 2002.

56   "What is a CVGA Certification?" Value Opportunity Profile online. Accessed September 6, 2020. https://www.corporatevalue.net/cvga.

57   "The Harvard MBA Business School Study on Goal Setting." Wanderlust Worker. Accessed September 9, 2020. www.wanderlustworker.com/the-harvard-mba-business-school-study-on-goal-setting/.

58   Tremendous Leadership. "About Being Tremendous." 2008. www.tremendousleadership.com/pages/Charlie/.

59   Burg, Bob, and John David Mann. "The Go-Giver: A Little Story About a Powerful Business Idea." The Go-Giver. 2007. www.thegogiver.com/wp-content/uploads/2015/08/The-5-Law.pdf.

60   Ibid.

61   Ibid.

62   Ibid.

63   Colan, Lee. "A Lesson from Roy A. Disney on Making Values-Based Decisions." Inc. July 24, 2019. www.inc.com/lee-colan/a-lesson-from-roy-a-disney-on-making-values-based-decisions.html.

64   Lenzner, Robert. "Bernie Madoff's $50 Billion Ponzi Scheme." Forbes, December 12, 2008. www.forbes.com/2008/12/12/madoff-ponzi-hedge-pf-ii-in_rl_1212croesus_inl.html?sh=13309a15650b.

65   Clarke, Suzan. "Chick-Fil-A Franchisee Gives Needy Man Free Meal, His Own Gloves." ABC News. January 13, 2015. www.abcnews.go.com/US/chick-fil-franchisee-needy-man-free-meal-gloves/story?id=28182111.

66   Friesner, Tim. "History of SWOT Analysis." Research Gate. January 2011. https://www.researchgate.net/publication/288958760_History_of_swot_analysis.

67   White, Malcolm. "Back to the Future: Rosser Reeves' Legacy." WARC. December 4, 2016. www.warc.com/newsandopinion/opinion/back-to-the-future-rosser-reeves-legacy/2265.

68   Exit Planning Institute. "CEPA Spotlight: Justin Goodbread." October 25, 2019. www.exit-planning-institute.org/blog/cepa-spotlight-justin-goodbread/.

69   Ophanian, Lee. "California Businesses Leave the State by the Thousands." Hoover. September 8, 2020. www.hoover.org/research/california-business-leave-state-thousands.

70   Baker, Scott R., et al. "The Unprecedented Stock Market Reaction to COVID-19." Becker Friedman Institute for Economics at U Chicago. June 2020. www.bfi.uchicago.edu/wp-content/uploads/BFI_White-Paper_Davis_3.2020.pdf.

71   Tabaka, Marla. "New Study Says This Simple Step Will Increase the Odds of Achieving Your Goals (Substantially)." Inc. January 28, 2019. www.inc.com/marla-tabaka/this-study-found-1-simple-step-to-practically-guarantee-youll-achieve-your-goals-for-real.html.

72   Stern, Joanna. "Jeff Bezos: A Down-to-Earth CEO Reaching for the Stars." ABC News. September 24, 2013. www.abcnews.go.com/Technology/jeff-bezos-amazons-earth-ceo-reaches-stars/story?id=20363682.

73   "Value Disciplines: Customer Intimacy, Product Leadership, and Operational Excellence." Business to You. October 23, 2018. www.business-to-you.

com/value-disciplines-customer-intimacy/.

74   Brodo, Robert. "Walmart's Strategic Financial Management Tactics." Advantexe. November 4, 2015. www.advantexe.com/blog/walmarts-strategic-financial-management-tactics.

75   "Introduction to Bowman's Strategy Clock." Lucidity. 2020. www.getlucidity.com/strategy-resources/introduction-to-bowmans-strategy-clock/.

76   "Introduction to the Ansoff Matrix." Lucidity. 2020. www.getlucidity.com/strategy-resources/introduction-to-ansoff-matrix/.

77   Kaplan, Robert S, and David P Norton. "The Balanced Scorecard-Measures That Drive Performance." Harvard Business Review, 1992. www.hbr.org/1992/01/the-balanced-scorecard-measures-that-drive-performance-2.

78   Kaplan, Robert S, and David P Norton. "Having Trouble with Your Strategy? Then Map It." Harvard Business Review, September 1, 2000. www.hbr.org/2000/09/having-trouble-with-your-strategy-then-map-it.

79   Eliason, Nathaniel. "The E-Myth by Michael Gerber: Summary, Notes, and Lessons." Nate Eliason. 2020. www.nateliason.com/notes/e-myth-michael-gerber.